The Jodie Davis Needle Arts School

♦ **THE FOUNDATION PIECING LIBRARY** ♦

VICTORIAN QUILT
BLOCK DESIGNS

The Jodie Davis
Needle Arts School

♦ THE FOUNDATION PIECING LIBRARY ♦

VICTORIAN QUILT BLOCK DESIGNS

JODIE DAVIS

DESIGNS BY LINDA HAMPTON SCHIFFER

FRIEDMAN/FAIRFAX

P U B L I S H E R S

A FRIEDMAN/FAIRFAX BOOK

© 1996 by Michael Friedman Publishing Group, Inc.

Library of Congress Cataloging-in-Publication data available upon request.

ISBN 1-56799-258-7

Project Editor: Elizabeth Viscott Sullivan
Editor: Eleanor Levie
Art Director: Jeff Batzli
Designer: Tanya Ross-Hughes
Photography Director: Christopher C. Bain
Production Associate: Marnie Ann Boardman

Photography by Christopher C. Bain
Illustrations by Barbara Hennig

Color separations by Excel Graphic Arts Limited
Printed in the United Kingdom by Butler and Tanner Limited

For bulk purchases and special sales, please contact:
Friedman/Fairfax Publishers
Attention: Sales Department
15 West 26th Street
New York, New York 10010
212/685-6610   FAX 212/685-1307

DEDICATION

To my family who supported me and to my paternal grandmother, Edna Mae Pennington Hampton, who
taught me my first stitches as a tiny girl.

CONTENTS

INTRODUCTION

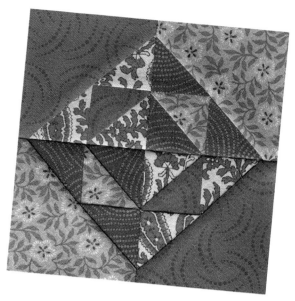

WHAT IS FOUNDATION PIECING?

Foundation piecing is simply the fastest and by far the easiest method ever devised for constructing quilt blocks—so easy, in fact, that even a complete beginner can make beautiful blocks. It's foolproof!

THE PROCESS IN A NUTSHELL

The blocks are constructed by sewing along lines marked on a paper or fabric foundation. The foundation provides stability, the lines accuracy.

First, the block design is transferred to the foundation. With the marked lines face up, two pieces of fabric, right sides together, are placed under the foundation and stitched to the foundation along a marked line. The two fabric pieces are pressed open, into place. More pieces are added until the block is complete. Finally, the blocks are sewn together. Voilà—a completed quilt top!

THE PATTERNS

The patterns included in this book come from a number of sources. Many are tried-and-true traditional patterns, popular with quilters since the mid-nineteenth century. Others are Linda's own designs;

some are variations on tradition, others her own inspired interpretations of the tastes of the times.

All the block designs are rated for ease of construction, designated by the number of diamonds appearing on the pattern page. If you are just beginning, select a pattern from those featuring one diamond. The more challenging patterns found in this book have three diamonds.

Foundation pieced blocks are the perfect opportunity for you to use those precious scraps you've been saving. And remember not to limit yourself to the block sizes that are offered in the book. Foundation piecing can make quick and perfect work out of any size block.

THE QUILTS

Twelve quilt designs, each using one or more of the patterns from the Quilt Block Patterns section, are offered in the Quilt Design section. These quilts provide the perfect opportunity to put your new skills to use in creating a finished project.

What could be easier? No templates, no marking, no painstaking cutting. Foundation piecing is easy enough for a beginner, yet challenges the seasoned quilter. Above all, foundation piecing offers accuracy and speed. And it's fun!

JODIE DAVIS

◆ CHAPTER ONE ◆

FOUNDATION
PIECING PRIMER

This chapter provides all the information you need to make the quilt blocks shown in this book. The only requirement is that you can sew along a straight line either by hand or with your sewing machine. That's it!

CALLING ALL HAND PIECERS

These patterns make excellent carry-along projects for trips, waiting rooms, and after-school practice waits. Transferred to fabric foundations, they can be easily executed by hand sewing. Only a few sewing supplies and small scraps are needed.

For hand piecing, choose a fabric foundation. Avoid paper—it's too difficult to sew through by hand.

You will be sewing from the wrong side of the blocks. The marked side of the foundation is the

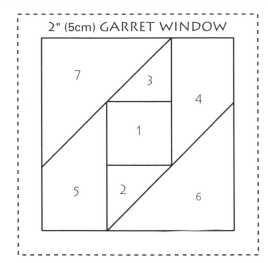

wrong side. For this reason the finished block will be a mirror image of the drawn designs in this book. Notice that the photos of the block are in fact mirror images of the drawn block. This is true for asymmetrical blocks. For symmetrical blocks, there will be no difference between the drawn and sewn blocks.

THE DESIGNS

The block and border designs in this book are full-size, and all are ready to be traced and used. Most are shown in 2" (5cm) and 4" (10cm) versions. The numbers on the blocks indicate the sewing sequence for the fabric pieces.

The lines on the block designs represent the sewing lines. A dashed ¼" (6mm) seam allowance has been added all around the outside of each block.

NOTE: If you use a photocopier to enlarge a block to another size, you'll need to redraw the seam allowance so it's ¼" (6mm).

Asymmetrical block

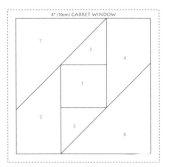

Symmetrical block

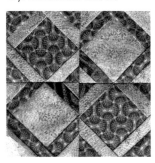
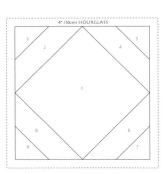

CREATIVE OPTIONS: For exciting and unusual quilts, play with block orientation and combinations. Look at the patterns, their mirror (flipped) images, and combinations of both. Plan for the final block/quilt design that you want. To do this easily, use a photocopy machine to make several copies of the selected block pattern, then arrange and rearrange these paper blocks until you like the result.

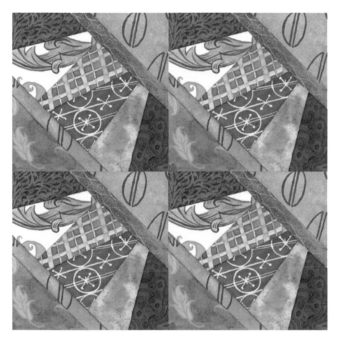

FOUNDATION OPTIONS

Foundations can be either permanent or temporary, depending upon the desired end result or working method (hand versus machine).

PERMANENT FOUNDATIONS

A fabric foundation is permanent. The patchwork pieces are stitched to the base fabric, which is usually muslin. The foundation then becomes an additional layer in the quilt sandwich. A benefit for some projects (for instance, to add body to a wall hanging or vest), a fabric foundation isn't the best choice in others, such as a project that calls for extensive hand quilting, or a miniature that shouldn't be too stiff.

Choose good quality muslin for your foundations, and be sure to prewash, especially if the finished project will be laundered.

> **Use the Olfa 6" [15cm] square template to cut perfectly square fabric foundations of any size.**
> ELEANOR LEVIE, DARIEN, CT

NOTE: When using a fabric foundation, cut the foundation square with the grainline of the fabric.

TEMPORARY FOUNDATIONS

Paper of many types is an excellent, inexpensive foundation. It provides more stability for piecing than muslin and eliminates the additional layer of a permanent fabric foundation, allowing for easier hand quilting. After construction, the paper is removed from the completed block by tearing. In some cases, this can cause fraying of seam allowances and distortion of the block; also, some bits of paper may remain stuck in the stitches. Avoid these problems by using a shorter stitch length. This way, removing the paper will be similar to tearing postage stamps apart.

Almost any paper is appropriate for foundation piecing. Copy, computer, and typing paper are readily available. Freezer paper, available in grocery stores, is a favorite of many quilters. The dull side can be marked with the block pattern and the shiny side pressed to fabric with a dry iron and a press cloth. Tracing paper has the advantage of lighter weight, so stitches won't distort as readily when the paper is torn away.

When making paper foundation patterns, whether on computer or by hand, I like to print on newsprint. This has two advantages: it tears easily, and it is porous enough that the ink shows through a tiny bit to the back of the paper. This makes placement of fabric pieces much easier.
AUDI GERSTEIN

I print my foundation patterns onto newsprint paper in my laser printer. I got the newsprint at a local paper warehouse. It comes precut 8½" × 11" [21×28cm] and is cheap! Very easy to tear away from the block.
SUSAN DRUDING, BERKELEY, CA

Here's a tip to make your paper removal easier. After you stitch a seam, score the paper at the seam while trimming. Then when you're ready to remove the paper, dampen the paper slightly with a sponge or spray it once with a fine spray. This will make your paper removal much easier! Don't get it too wet. If you do, then just press it a bit with a warm iron.
Or use a cheap-grade typing paper or onionskin paper, and press the finished block to scorch the paper. The paper becomes brittle and you can practically "snap" it off!
ANNIE TOTH, MOORPARK, CA

TRANSFERRING THE BLOCK DESIGNS

To reproduce the block designs on paper, trace or photocopy the desired pattern from the book. When tracing, use a ruler to ensure accuracy. Be sure to copy the piecing sequence numbers as well.

A copy machine makes quick work of reproducing patterns. To test the precision of the copies, make one copy of a block and measure it against the original to be sure the size is correct.

Cut along the outside dash lines.

To transfer the block designs to fabric, you may place the muslin over the block design on a light table or tape the design to a sunny window. Trace using fabric-permanent tools. As an alternative, use heat transfer pens or pencils to speed the marking of fabric foundations. Following the manufacturer's instructions, make a transfer on paper and check it for accuracy. You can then make multiple replicas on fabric or paper using the same transfer.

NOTE: Be sure to use marking tools such as pencil or permanent fabric pens when marking the fabric foundations. Pigma and Pilot SC-UF are good examples. If the ink used is not stable, it can bleed through the block front during construction or after the quilt is complete.

NOTE: Cut fabric foundations on the straight grain of the fabric.

BLOCKS IN ANY SIZE

If you require block sizes other than the two offered, start with the 4" (10cm) block and refer to the following chart to adjust the size; remember to adjust the seam allowances to ¼" (6mm) all around.

For a block size of:	Set the copy machine to:
3" (7.5cm)	75%
5" (12.5cm)	125%
6" (15cm)	150%
8" (20cm)	200%

FABRICS

Fabric shops offer a delicious variety of fabrics for the quilter. High-quality all-cotton fabrics used in traditional quilting are a joy to work with and have a timeless appeal.

Many quilters are exploring the possibilities of such nontraditional quilting fabrics as lamé, flannel, and unusual blends. For flimsy fabrics such as tissue lamé, fuse interfacing to the wrong side of the fabric before use (tricot-backed lamés are preferred as they don't fray, nor do they require backing with interfacing). A muslin foundation will give thin, delicate fabrics the extra support they require.

In choosing fabrics for the projects in this book, Linda selected from color palettes appropriate to the Victorian era. Today's hand-dyed and hand-painted fabrics work up into striking blocks and quilts as well and illustrate how well these patterns have stood the test of time.

PREPARING FABRICS

If you are using small scraps to make blocks, be sure the scrap is at least ¾" (2cm) larger than the final patch dimensions. If in doubt, put the fabric against the back of the marked foundation and hold it up to the light.

> A light box (my husband made me one for my birthday) is very helpful when foundation piecing. If I just can't eye up the fabrics holding them up to the light, I turn on the light box and can see the line/fabric every time. It is especially helpful for the darker fabrics which tend to just fade into the line on the other side.
> PATRICIA WILSON, SUNNYDALE, CA

For larger scraps or new yardage, cut strips at least ¾" (2cm) larger than the desired final patch. Or, cut strips 3" (7.5cm) wide (for 2" [5cm] blocks) or 6" (15cm) wide (for 4" [10cm] blocks); these can be cut across the length to fit specific patch spaces as needed.

SEWING

For paper piecing set your sewing machine to 18 to 20 stitches per inch (2.5cm) or a stitch setting of 1½, depending upon the make of your machine. The short stitch length creates closely spaced perforations which will facilitate tearing away the paper, if that is your choice of foundation. Simultaneously, it stabilizes the seam.

> Place a lamp near your sewing machine. Use this light source to place fabric pieces on your foundation. By holding the pieces up to the light, you will be able to see through all of the layers of fabric to check their alignment.

Use an 80/12 needle. If you use a paper foundation, switch to a 90/14 needle if you have trouble tearing the paper away.

Choose your thread color according to the fabrics selected. Light gray is a good choice for assorted lighter fabrics, dark gray when working with black prints and darker fabrics.

For final block assembly, use your normal stitch length.

FOUNDATION PIECING METHOD

To demonstrate the foundation piecing method, I have chosen one of the easiest blocks in the book as an example. Follow these steps to make your own practice block.

REMEMBER: The marked side of the foundation will be at the back of the finished block. Therefore, the finished block will be a mirror image of the drawn pattern.

> I key my paper foundations for easier and faster piecing. By coloring in the sections (1, 2, 3...) according to the fabrics that go there, I eliminate confusion and speed up my piecing.
>
> ELLEN ROBINSON, GERMANTOWN, MD

1. Beginning with the shape marked #1 on the pattern, place the fabric you've chosen for piece #1 with the wrong side against the unmarked side of the foundation paper or fabric. Hold the foundation

and fabric up to a source of light to help you see the marked lines. Pin in place. Make sure the fabric covers the shape with at least ¼" (6mm) extending over marked lines all around. Be generous with the fabric; it's better to have too big a piece now than to end up short later.

2. Cut a piece of fabric for piece #2. Since the back of the block design is facing you, hold the fabric wrong side up to cut it. Pin piece #2 against piece #1, right sides together and adjacent edges even. Working from the back, stitch along the marked line; begin and end the stitching a few stitches beyond the ends of the line.

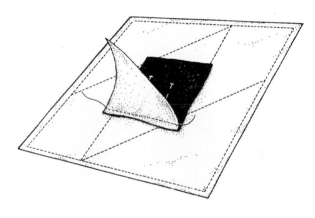

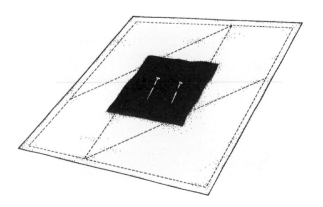

> If you have trouble seeing the marked line when sewing, switch to a transparent or open toe foot on your sewing machine.

3. Trim the seam allowances to ¼" (6mm). For blocks 2" (5cm) square or smaller, trim to ⅛" (3mm).

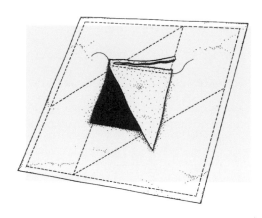

NOTE: Be careful not to cut the foundation when trimming seam allowances. Feel for the foundation with your fingers or scissors—or look. It will save you a lot of grief!

Fold piece #2 into place and finger press. Then, press with a dry iron—no steam.

4. In the same manner, add the third and all subsequent pieces, pressing as you go.

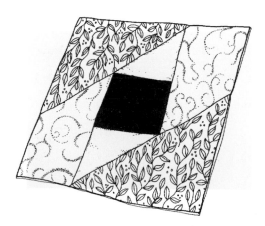

5. Using a rotary cutter and ruler or square template, trim the edges of the block. Leave a ¼" (6mm) seam allowance all the way around the block as indicated on the pattern by short dash lines.

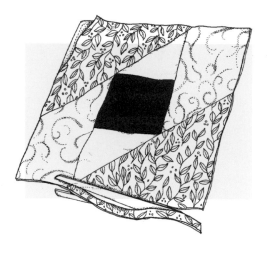

OPTIONAL: When using a permanent foundation, some quilters baste around the finished block from the right side, just inside the seam allowances. This anchors the fabric pieces so they won't move out of place when you're joining the blocks.

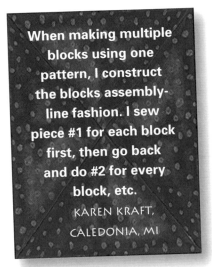

When making multiple blocks using one pattern, I construct the blocks assembly-line fashion. I sew piece #1 for each block first, then go back and do #2 for every block, etc.

KAREN KRAFT, CALEDONIA, MI

If you wish to center a special fabric motif or fill a shape evenly, be sure to check the alignment by holding the fabric and foundation up to the light.

> When making multiples of the same block, make an extra copy of the block. Glue appropriate fabric scraps in place and hang it where you can see it easily. This will guide you as you sew and will prevent mix-ups.

SUBUNIT BLOCKS

Several block patterns consist of two pieces, such as two triangles (subunits), each requiring a slightly different treatment. The two subunits are prepared using foundation piecing techniques, and then joined together to make a complete 2" (5cm) or 4" (10cm) block, matching points and seams where necessary.

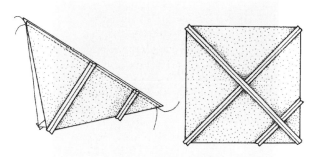

WHAT ABOUT THE GRAINLINE?

For all patchwork it is important to be aware of fabric grain considerations. Fabric is woven, and you can easily see the intersecting threads, or grainlines. The lengthwise grain (parallel to the selvedges) has less "give" or elasticity than the crosswise grain (perpendicular to the selvedges). If you pull a piece of fabric diagonally (at a 45-degree angle) to the grain, you will get a lot of stretching—this is the bias.

When you assemble patchwork blocks, you should be aware that putting bias edges along the outside edges of the block will allow the block to stretch easily. The resulting variance of edge lengths will hinder easy joining of the blocks and prevent your quilt from hanging or laying straight.

One of the real virtues of foundation piecing is that this concern with grainline can be minimized. If using a permanent fabric foundation, be sure your pattern is applied to the foundation fabric even with the grain lines. Then you will not need to be concerned at all with the grainline of any of the fabrics you use to piece your block. In addition, you can orient the printed pattern on your patch fabric to please your eye, with no concern for grain.

However, if you use a paper foundation and wish to remove the paper before final quilt top assembly, you need to be careful not to put bias edges along the outer seam lines of your blocks. You can leave the paper foundations on the blocks until after assembly to alleviate this worry over outer bias edges.

> Leave the paper foundation in place until after you join the blocks together. Blocks will be easier to align, and won't become distorted by tearing the paper away. This also eliminates concern about the grainline of the block edges.

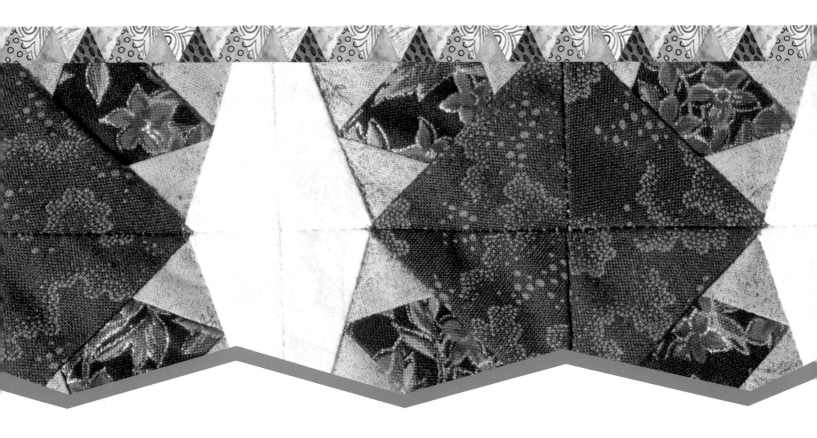

♦ CHAPTER TWO ♦

BLOCK PATTERNS

TRADITIONAL INFLUENCES

Many of the traditional patchwork and appliqué patterns we hold dear either came into being or became popular during the period of 1850 to 1915. This was an exciting period in American quilting history. Quilting flourished, much as it is doing now, with many new patterns, fabrics, and design approaches enjoying popularity. This was a period in America of great growth of population and geography, with the westward settlement and expansion of the nation. In addition, the explosion of urban growth and the accelerating effects of the Industrial Revolution enriched the options for materials and resources for the quilter. Needlework skills continued to be held in high regard and quiltmaking was a much-practiced art. The growth in literacy and urbanization fueled a corresponding increase in the publication of quilting patterns and needlework magazines. The availability of fabrics and designs by mail order, even to more remote rural areas, greatly increased. New ideas and innovations in quiltmaking could

be rapidly spread throughout the country, especially once the transcontinental railway connected both coasts of the growing nation.

The American centennial celebrations in 1876 prompted many quilters to produce commemorative quilts, and special centennial commemorative fab-

rics were printed by several companies. Many patriotic quilts were made during this period, and patterns incorporating star motifs abounded. The widespread establishment of public education produced one of the most popular of all American design families, the Little Red Schoolhouse. The Log Cabin family of patterns became increasingly popular as the country was more urbanized; in sections of the country still being settled, these patterns were prized for their clever use of scraps. Growing trade with the Orient inspired vastly popular fads for crazy patchwork and silk fabric use in quiltmaking, with such designs as Baby Blocks and Mosaic patterns (one of which we more commonly call Grandmother's Flower Garden today) remaining popular. Patterns requiring real skill to execute, such as Ocean Waves, Lady of the Lake, various counterpoint designs, and elaborate floral appliqués, were prized and became more common as leisure time increased for the middle class.

Industrialization allowed many young women to earn their own wages and thus afford goods for the inevitable dowry quilts. Increased emphasis on social and civic participation encouraged the rise in fund-raising quilts, many of the subscription signature variety. The women's rights and suffrage movements fostered the making of politically expressive quilts, quilts to donate for charity, and quilts for raffle or fund-raising purposes.

Textile mills responded to the increase in demand for quilt fabrics by printing a wide variety of colors and designs of cotton fabrics. With the advent of the use of artificial dyes, a much wider range of colors could be produced to add to the already popular indigo, Turkey red, green, and chocolate brown prints. Late Victorian quilts are filled with brilliant "chrome" oranges, greens, purples, and so on.

The block patterns selected for this book celebrate this exciting period in American history. From the unassuming everyday patterns in Farmhouse Best to the civic-minded designs in Patriotic Fever,

each pattern holds the memories of many hands and hearts. Create your own bit of history with these patterns, using the wonderfully labor-saving and accurate foundation piecing method—certainly a concept of which our hardworking forbears would approve!

This chapter, the heart of the book, is a library of designs. Each section includes color photographs of the quilt blocks stitched up in fabric.

Next, a page is devoted to each of the blocks. Each block pattern, including numbers denoting the order in which the block is to be constructed, appears actual-size. In addition, a watercolor of each block shows variations in the ways the blocks can be put together to form quilt patterns. These ideas are intended to illustrate the versatility of the designs and to give you inspiration for your own quilts.

LINDA HAMPTON SCHIFFER

For more information about the quiltmaking history of the Victorian era, read Kiracofe's *The American Quilt* or Barbara Brackman's *Clues in the Calico* (see Bibliography).

PATTERN COMMENTS

◆ = 1 diamond (easy)
◆◆ = 2 diamonds (modest difficulty)
◆◆◆ = 3 diamonds (challenging)

CRAZY PASSIONS

Perhaps inspired by an exhibit of traditional Japanese garments, the crazy patchwork fad swept the Victorian world. Many women enthusiastically embraced the chance to make an individualized work of art and show off their multiple needlework and quilting talents. These patterns offer a chance for modern quilters to further the tradition by experimenting with unusual fabrics and threads, rubber-stamped and photo-transferred images, hand inking, beading, and embroidery.

NOTE: All blocks are shown with ¼" (6mm) seam allowance.

BEGGAR BLOCK ◆

Confining the crazy patchwork within the body of this simple pattern allows you to use coordinating colors on the border. You can impose order and a "resting place" for the eye by choosing your corner fabrics carefully.

CRAZY PIECES ◆◆◆

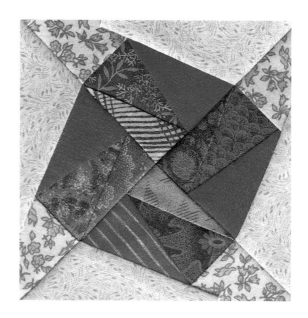

Unlike most crazy patchwork, this pattern makes a recognizable design, in this case a whirling star. Four subunits make one block. Though this block requires more assembly than some patterns, the final effect is worth the extra work. Accentuate the star by choosing bright scraps for its blades and trailers.

These easy blocks were loosely based on four from an antique crazy patchwork quilt made around 1870 by Elizabeth Parkhurst Williams. You can see the striking original on page 147 of Kiracofe's *The American Quilt.*

CRAZY I, II, III, IV ◆

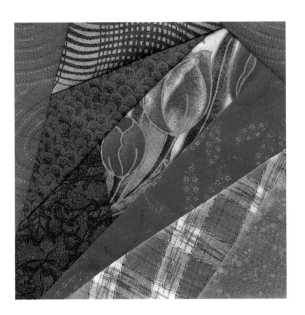

BEGGAR BLOCK

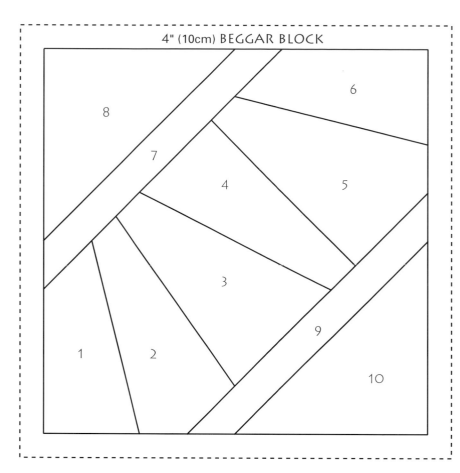

4" (10cm) BEGGAR BLOCK

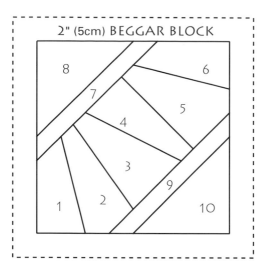

2" (5cm) BEGGAR BLOCK

Creative options

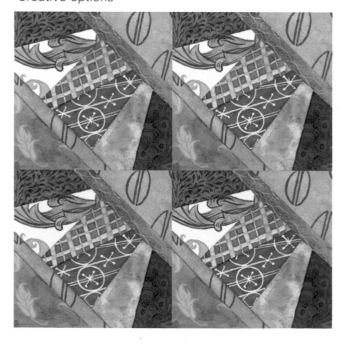

CRAZY PIECES

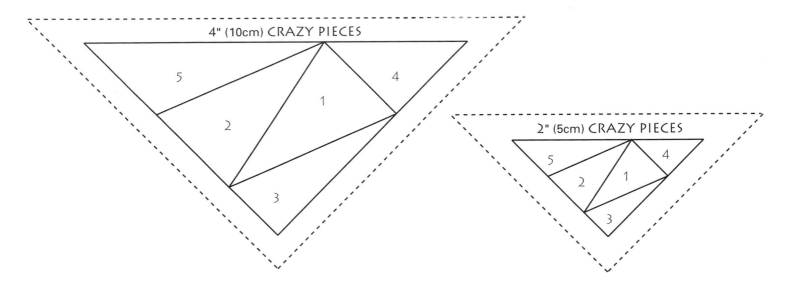

4" (10cm) CRAZY PIECES

2" (5cm) CRAZY PIECES

Creative option

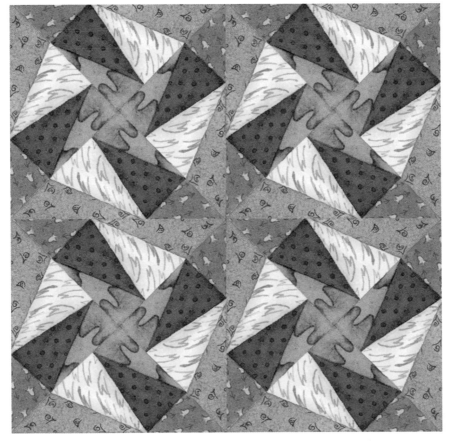

4" (10cm) CRAZY PATCH I

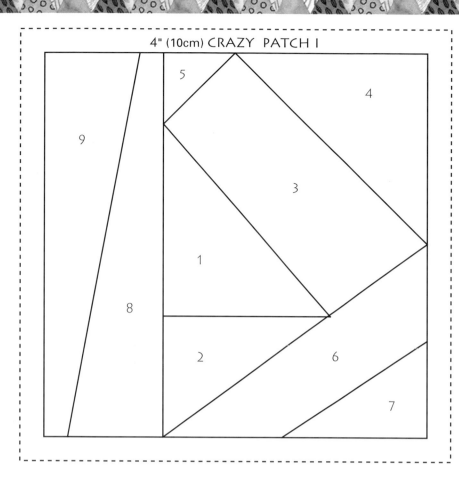

2" (5cm) CRAZY PATCH I

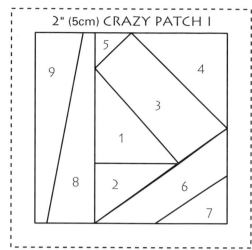

4" (10cm) CRAZY PATCH II

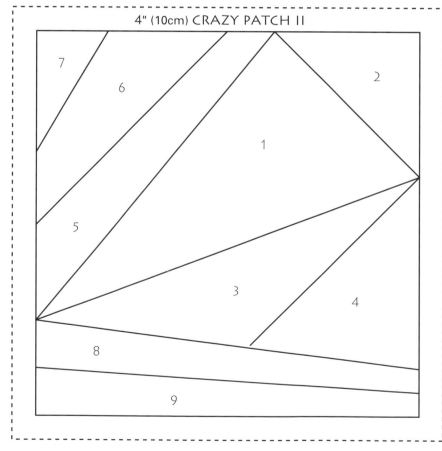

2" (5cm) CRAZY PATCH II

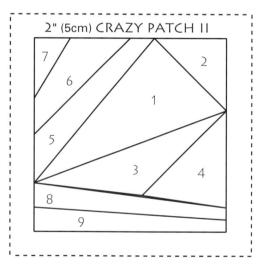

4" (10cm) CRAZY PATCH III

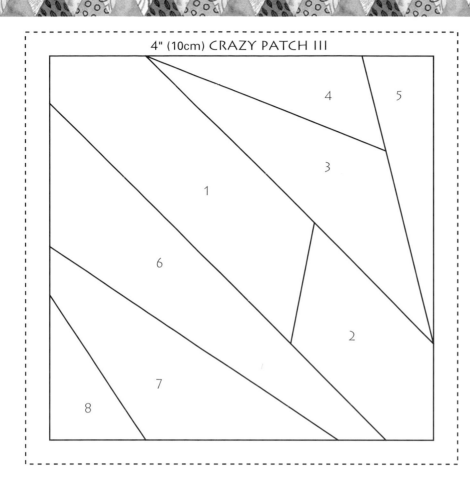

2" (5cm) CRAZY PATCH III

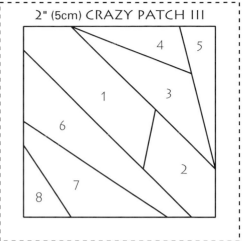

4" (10cm) CRAZY PATCH IV

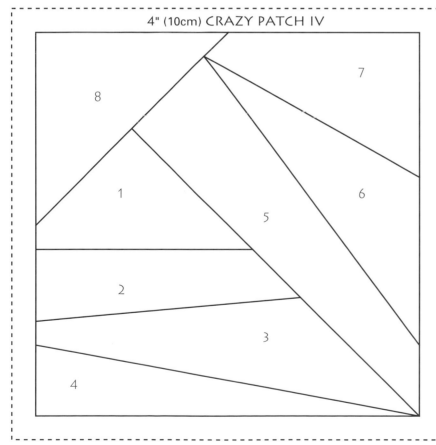

2" (5cm) CRAZY PATCH IV

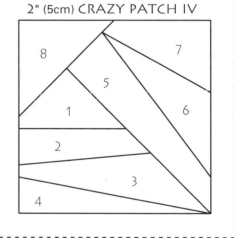

ORIENTAL WONDER

Increased trade with the Orient inspired many Victorian needleworkers to explore their own versions of Eastern pattern motifs. Imported pottery, fabrics, and home furnishings sparked an entirely new design aesthetic that quilters assimilated into their art form. The resulting patterns, fabric design, and color schemes enriched the quilter's arsenal and were used to great effect.

Today fabric shops offer time-honored historic prints as well as modern Oriental-inspired fabrics. A quilt stitched from a selection of Japanese block printed indigo cottons is smashing in its subtlety—the successful marriage of Oriental fabrics and Americanized design. Continuing this tradition, fabric designers routinely create a variety of gorgeous fabrics of Eastern design influence. Luscious color abounds, and the use of metallic gold sparkles on quilt tops.

Enjoy these blocks, whether you choose traditional Japanese indigo fabrics of contemporary Oriental prints. Or strike out in a different direction: wouldn't a fan design be lovely stitched from silk ties?

KIMONO ◆◆

This kimono has a bit more detail than most patterns, and so allows for more interest in the final "garment." A good pattern in which to feature those special fabric motifs you love, it requires subunit assembly.

CHINESE PUZZLE ◆◆

This traditional pattern will make a variety of interesting overall design layouts. Experiment! The assembly

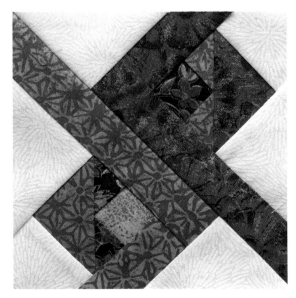

of the two subunit pieces is very easy and requires no matching of points with the triangular block.

GENTLEMAN'S FAN ◆

This is an easy block of the "paddle" fan variety. Not overly feminine in shape, it can be dressed up or down depending on your fabric selection.

SAMURAI FAN ◆◆

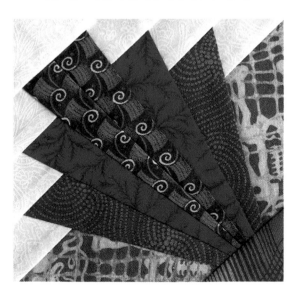

This block is actually very easy to do and requires no seam matching to assemble. You can choose very bold or traditional colors to make it striking. Corner triangles #8 and #9 are added after the two triangles are joined. Two subunits create one block.

MILADY'S FAN ◆

The folding fan was invented in Japan and was a part of every courtier's required costuming for centuries. We think of fans as a lady's accessory, useful for flirtation as well as decoration. This is an easy pattern to work despite its complex angles.

KIMONO

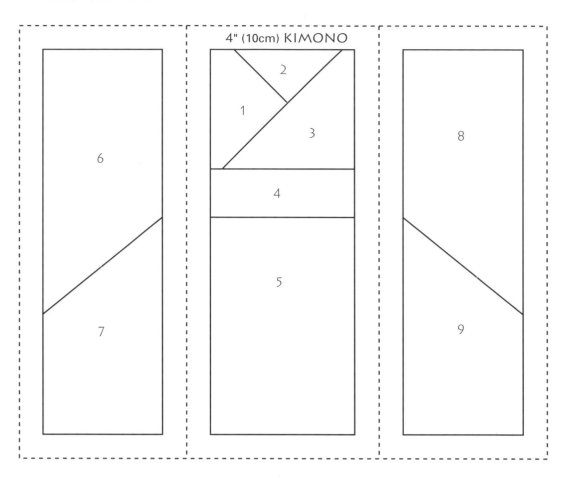

4" (10cm) KIMONO

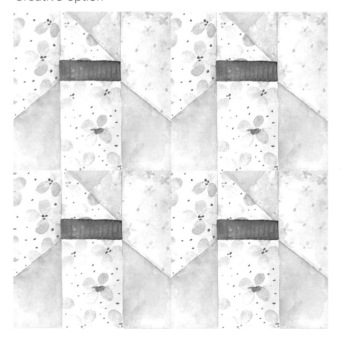

Creative option

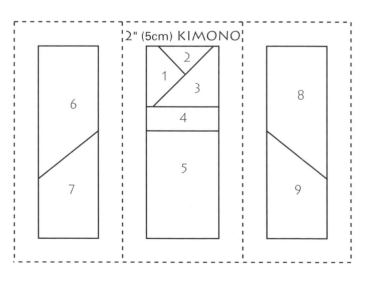

2" (5cm) KIMONO

CHINESE PUZZLE

4" (10cm) CHINESE PUZZLE

5
2
7
9
4
1
3
8
6

2" (5cm) CHINESE PUZZLE

5
2
7
9
4
1
3
8
6

Creative options

GENTLEMAN'S FAN

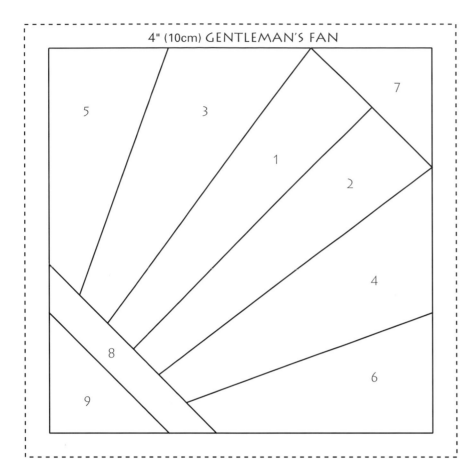

4" (10cm) GENTLEMAN'S FAN

2" (5cm) GENTLEMAN'S FAN

Creative options

SAMURAI FAN

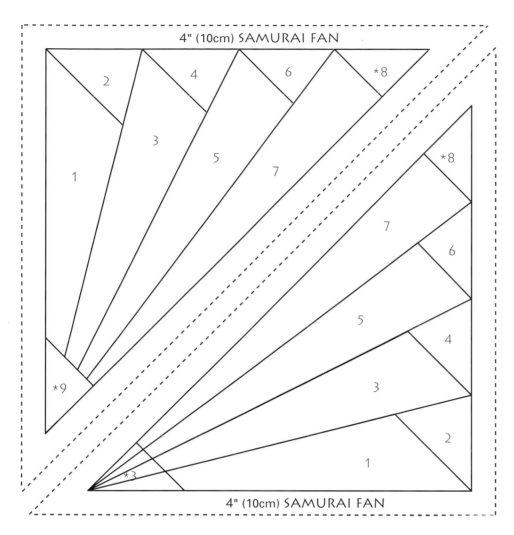

4" (10cm) SAMURAI FAN

4" (10cm) SAMURAI FAN

Creative option

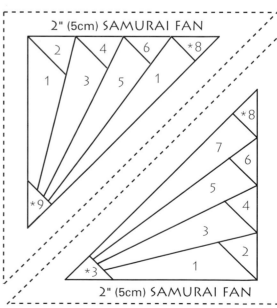

2" (5cm) SAMURAI FAN

2" (5cm) SAMURAI FAN

MILADY'S FAN

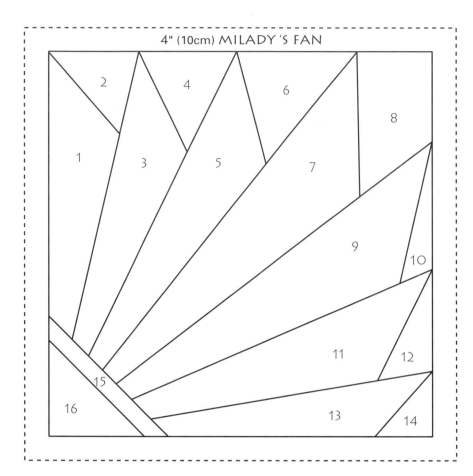

4" (10cm) MILADY'S FAN

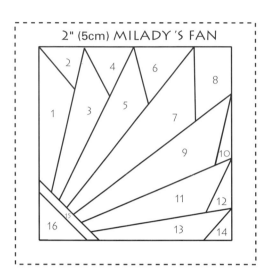

2" (5cm) MILADY'S FAN

Creative option

FRONT PARLOR FANCY

This assortment of patterns represents those found on "good" quilts, which were saved for "show." Enjoy making these and be proud to exhibit your resulting works of art.

ROSEBUD ◆◆

First published by the Ladies Art Circle in the late 1890s, this pattern can make interesting overall designs. It requires four subunits to produce one block, but there are no matching points to worry over until you join the blocks.

challenging, it can be used for many interesting optical effects. Be sure to experiment with mirror images and various block layout combinations.

CROSS AND CROWN ◆◆

This is a variant of a favored traditional pattern, first published by Ladies Art Circle around 1889. Choose different center "sash" fabrics for spice.

PALM FROND ◆◆◆

A three-leaved variant of a favorite traditional block, this pattern was first published in 1901 by the Ladies Art Circle. Four subunits make one block. Though

PINEBURR BEAUTY ◆◆◆

This block is slightly more challenging as it requires matching points to assemble the subunits. Four sub-units make one block. Look carefully at your choice of background fabrics if you decide on an overall block layout—you can achieve some exciting contemporary effects.

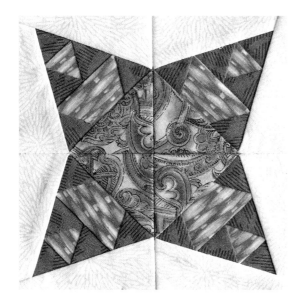

DELECTABLE MOUNTAINS ◆

Delectable Mountains has been a favorite patchwork pattern for more than a hundred years, appealing to old-time traditional quilters and contemporary fabric

CROCUS ◆

This very easy flower pattern is homage to the many beloved red, white, and green floral quilts made in the last century. Careful shade choices of fabrics for the petals will give depth to the blossom.

artists alike. Here, the tedious "feather" points have been reduced to an easy foundation block. Experiment with different block layouts; many variations exist.

ROSEBUD

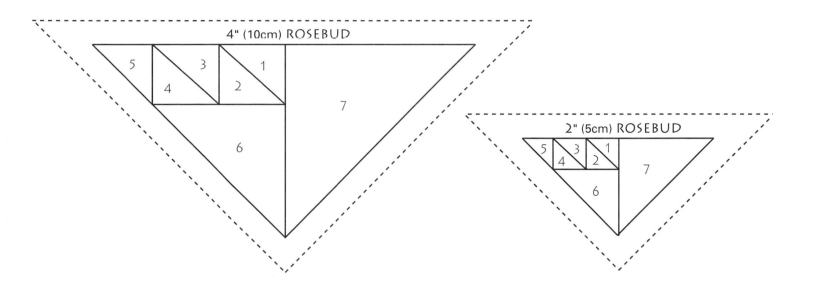

4" (10cm) ROSEBUD

2" (5cm) ROSEBUD

Creative options

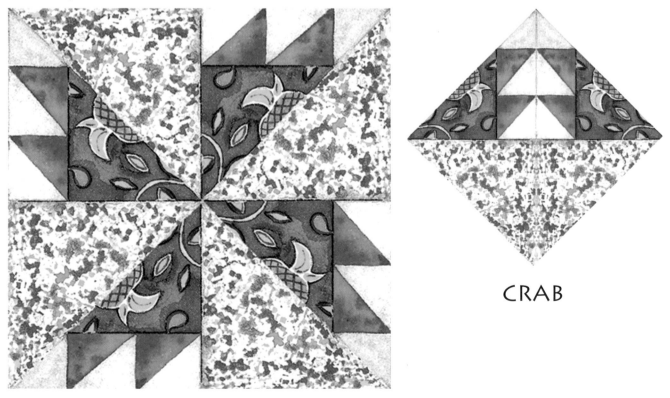

CRAB

PALM FROND

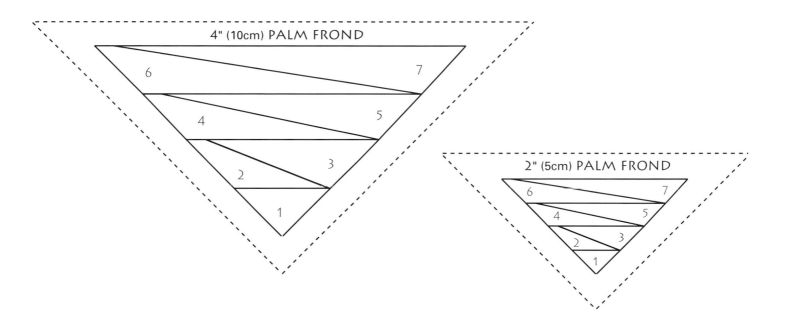

4" (10cm) PALM FROND

2" (5cm) PALM FROND

Creative options

CROSS AND CROWN

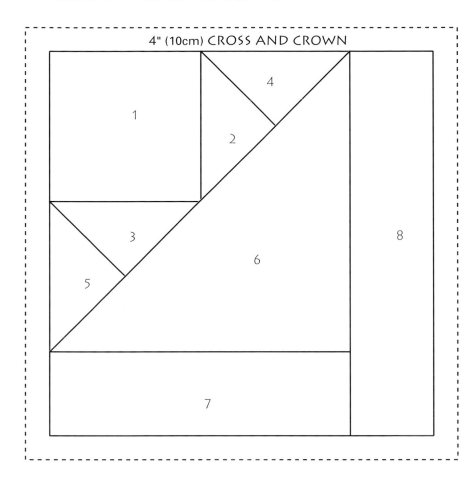

4" (10cm) CROSS AND CROWN

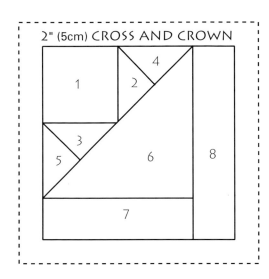

2" (5cm) CROSS AND CROWN

Creative options

PINEBURR BEAUTY

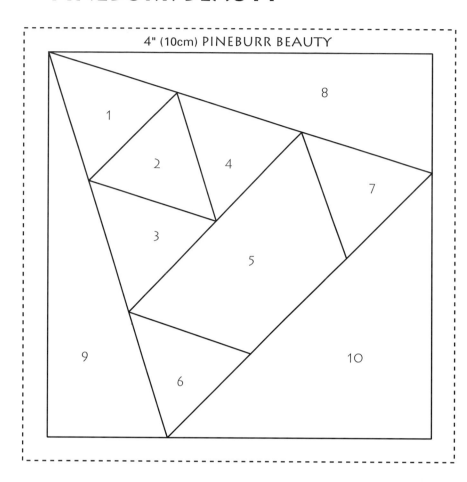

4" (10cm) PINEBURR BEAUTY

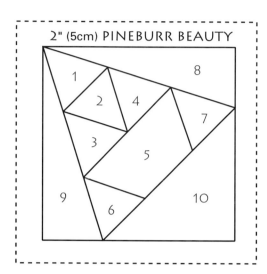

2" (5cm) PINEBURR BEAUTY

Creative option

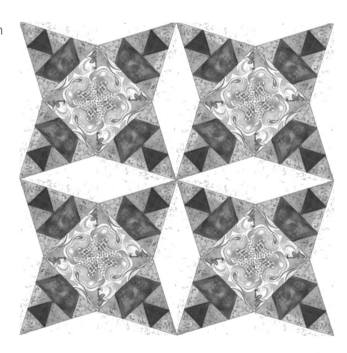

CROCUS

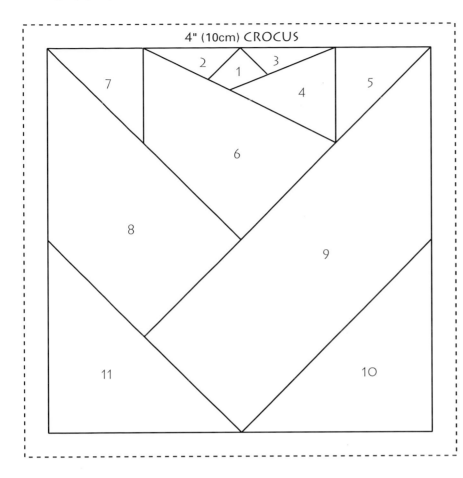

4" (10cm) CROCUS

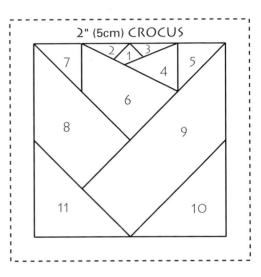

2" (5cm) CROCUS

Creative options

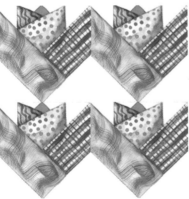

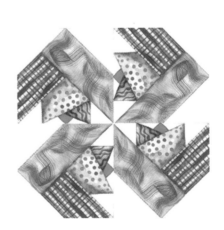

DELECTABLE MOUNTAINS

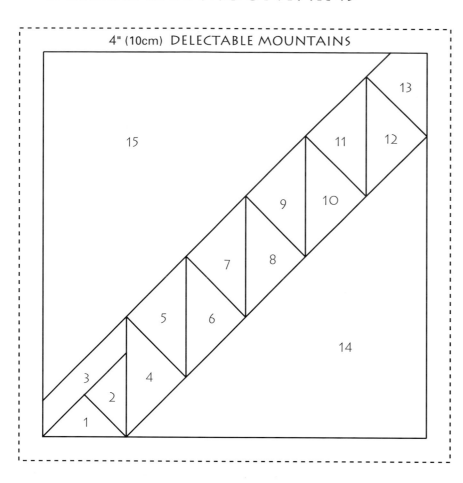

4" (10cm) DELECTABLE MOUNTAINS

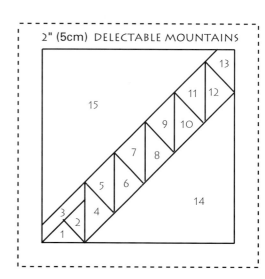

2" (5cm) DELECTABLE MOUNTAINS

Creative option

FARMHOUSE BEST

The scrap quilts produced for daily use by frugal farm women and city wives alike were often the most beloved objects in the home. Out of necessity the fabrics used for utility quilts were most likely the remains from clothing construction, with not even the smallest scrap wasted. After being altered and passed down to a smaller sibling, clothing fabric in good shape was recycled once more. Cut up into pieces for quilts, sister's first school dress and mother's blue-flowered apron were stitched into a quilt along with the memories of the family.

Take a cue from the housewives of old: don't be afraid to take a chance in your fabric choices for your keepsake quilt. Choose delicate and bold prints in various scales: throw in a fabric with an allover print and even a stripe. For a bit of fun, consider a dash of plaid. Often overlooked today, plaid leftovers from shirts of years ago made their way into scrap bags and quilts—and to great effect.

Pull out your scraps and tidbits and enjoy a playful experiment with color, pattern, and texture while making these designs. The result may be a "homey" quilt in the best sense.

NOTE: If you use older, worn fabrics, they may need some extra support. A fabric foundation will help, or fuse lightweight interfacing to their backs.

INTERLACED STAR ◆◆

This patchwork pattern is a personal favorite. It looks complex but is easy to assemble from four subunits for a block, several for a border. Play with color choices to achieve the interlaced look.

BABY BLOCKS ◆

This pattern was a popular one in Victorian times and is still popular today. There are many possible variants. You can easily assemble the subunits into rows. Color a layout design to experiment with stars and three-dimensional effects.

GARRET WINDOW ◆

This is a very easy traditional patchwork pattern, first published in *American Needlewoman*. It has some interesting layout variations—try these arrangements, as well as your own!

can see fish motifs, but Xs, hourglasses, and broken-dish patterns are also possibilities. This makes an excellent scrap quilt.

BUTTERFLIES ◆◆

Choose bright scraps for a lively finished quilt, full of fluttering wings. You'll find the subunit assembly very easy.

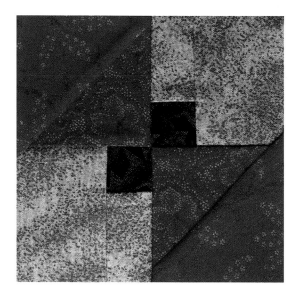

COUNTRY COUSINS ◆◆◆

This is a very basic patchwork block that will make many patterns. If you choose the right fabrics, you

INTERLACED STAR

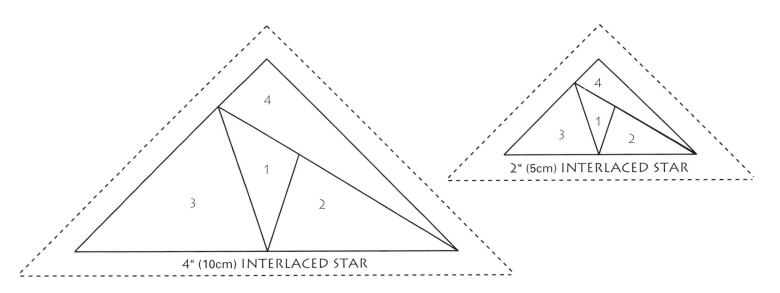

4" (10cm) INTERLACED STAR

2" (5cm) INTERLACED STAR

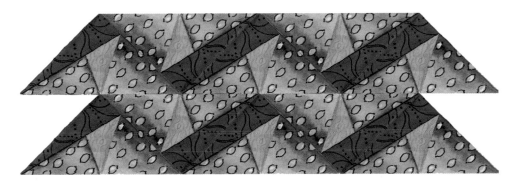

Creative options

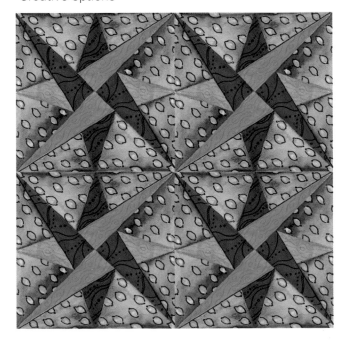

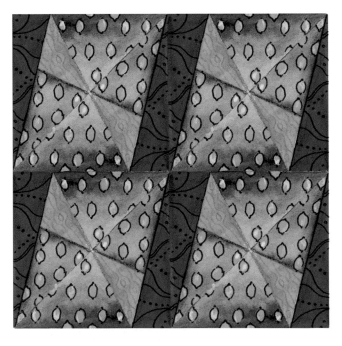

BABY BLOCKS

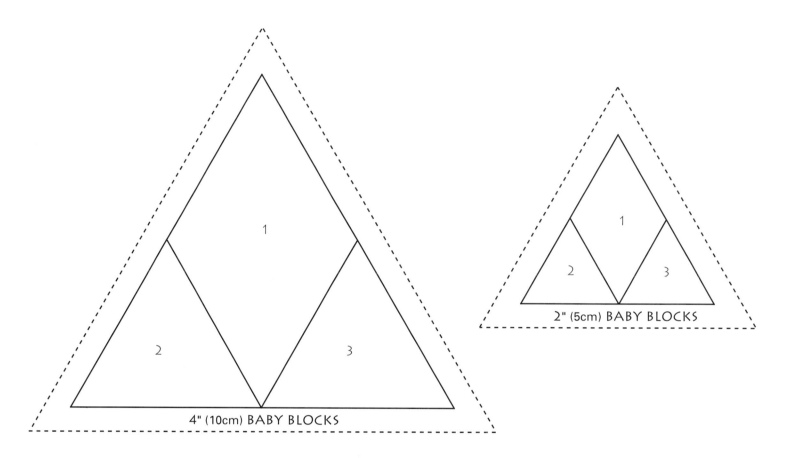

4" (10cm) BABY BLOCKS

2" (5cm) BABY BLOCKS

Creative options

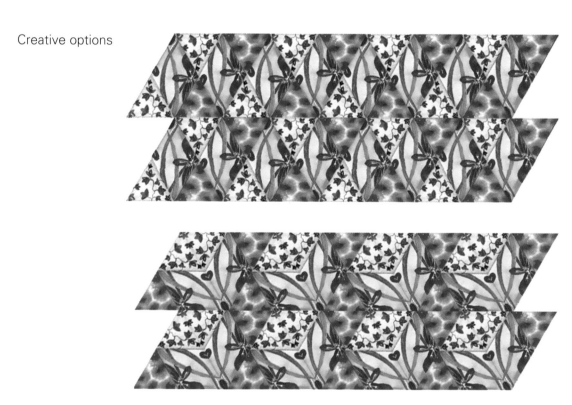

BABY BLOCK COLORING/DESIGN SHEET

GARRET WINDOW

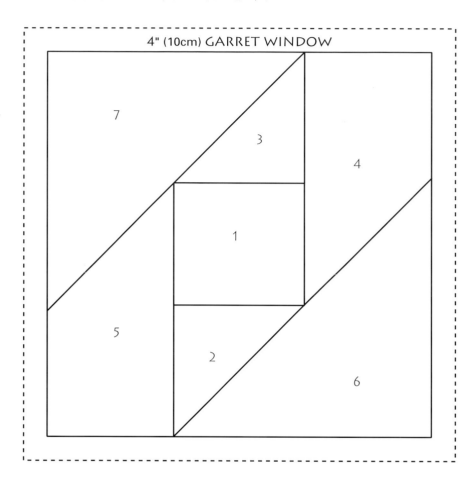

4" (10cm) GARRET WINDOW

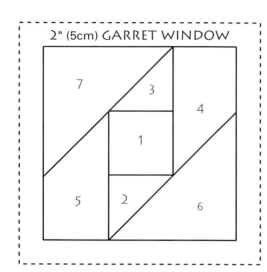

2" (5cm) GARRET WINDOW

Creative options

COUNTRY COUSINS

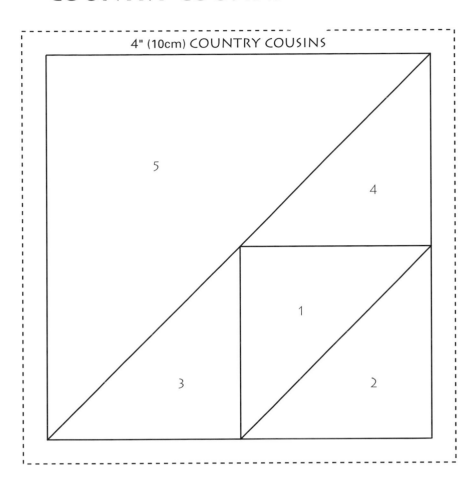

4" (10cm) COUNTRY COUSINS

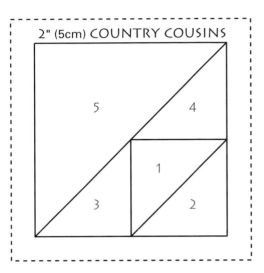

2" (5cm) COUNTRY COUSINS

Creative option

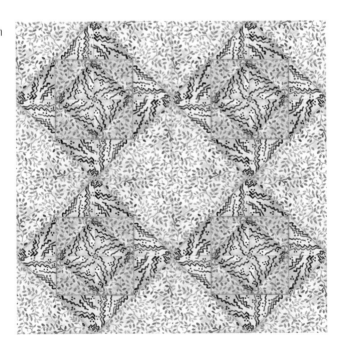

BUTTERFLIES

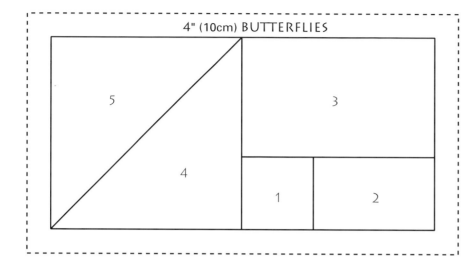

4" (10cm) BUTTERFLIES

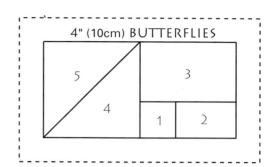

4" (10cm) BUTTERFLIES

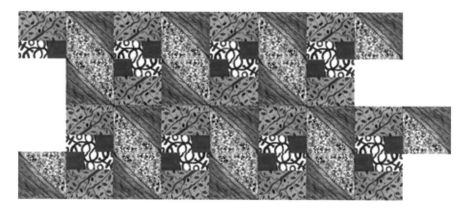

Creative options

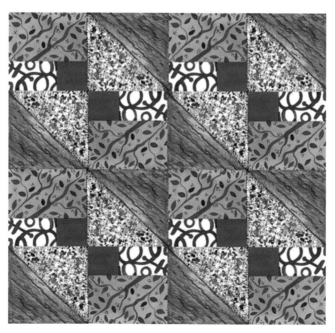

ROYAL VICTORIAN

Victorian needlewomen enjoyed displaying their skills with striking counterpoint designs. These patterns are sure to produce brilliant graphic quilts, eye-catching and impressive, to exhibit modern needle skills as well.

ANNA'S CHOICE ◆◆

A very simple block with an easy subunit assembly, this pattern is nevertheless striking in its positive/negative effects. Imagine one subunit alone for a kite design!

VARIABLE STAR ◆◆◆

This is a counterpoint version of the beloved Sawtooth Star or Ohio Star pattern. If the central star is colored from all the same fabrics, you will get a lovely Evening Star result. Despite the "variables" of piecing the two subunits, this one is worth the work.

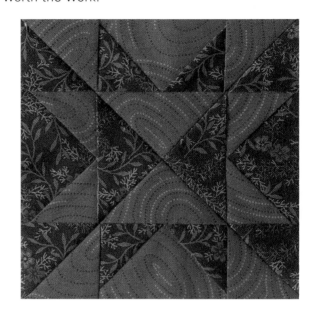

NIGHT AND DAY ◆◆◆

A beautiful counterpoint pattern. Careful fabric selection will make the stars appear three-dimensional and elegantly faceted, like a real gem.

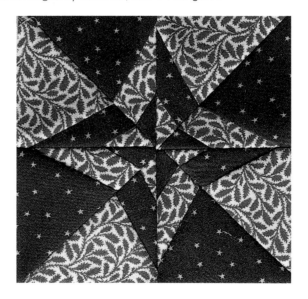

GRETCHEN ◆◆◆

Actually a simpler subunit assembly than some counterpoint patterns, this block offers some exciting diagonal movement when used in an overall block layout format.

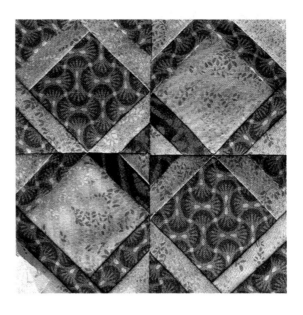

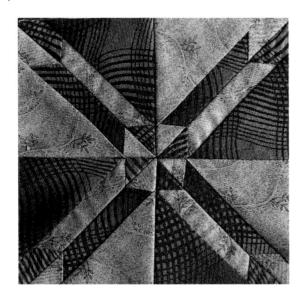

DOUBLE PINWHEEL ◆◆◆

This pattern of two subunits will yield striking overall effects when colored in counterpoint style. It's well worth the work of matching seams.

HOURGLASS ◆◆

This is an easy block to use for counterpoint coloring. The "hourglass" figures that result from matching the corners also look like the windings on spools of thread. Choose your fabrics to make the desired motifs stand out. This is traditionally made in red and white.

ANNA'S CHOICE

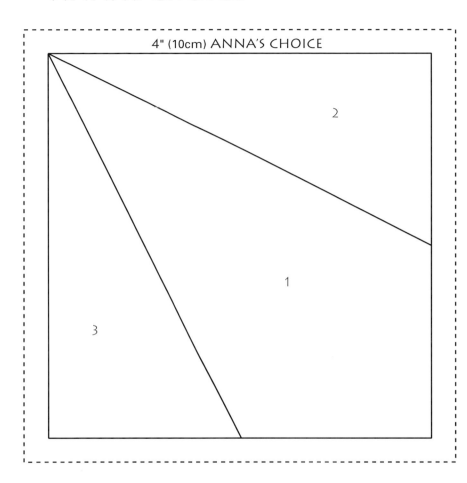

4" (10cm) ANNA'S CHOICE

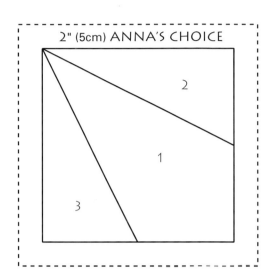

2" (5cm) ANNA'S CHOICE

Creative option

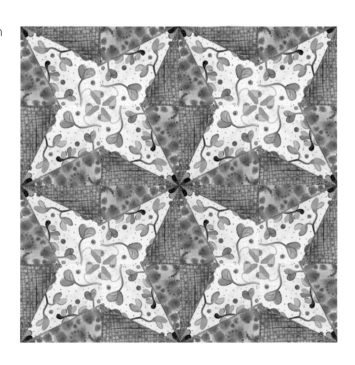

VARIABLE STAR

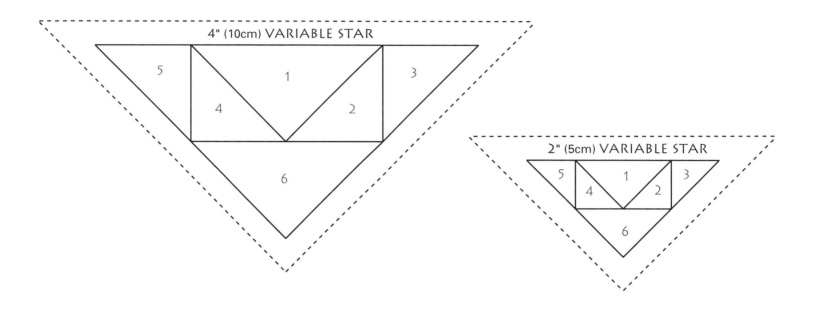

4" (10cm) VARIABLE STAR

2" (5cm) VARIABLE STAR

Creative option

NIGHT AND DAY

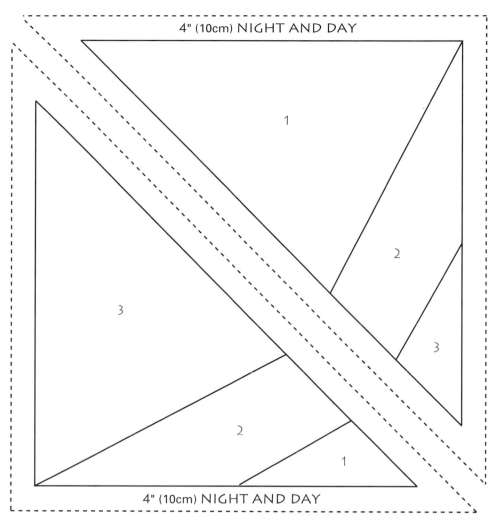

4" (10cm) NIGHT AND DAY

4" (10cm) NIGHT AND DAY

Creative option

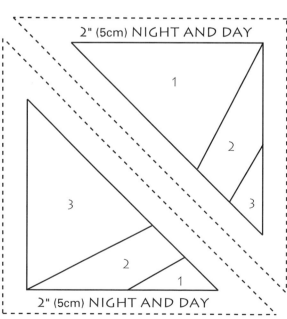

2" (5cm) NIGHT AND DAY

2" (5cm) NIGHT AND DAY

GRETCHEN

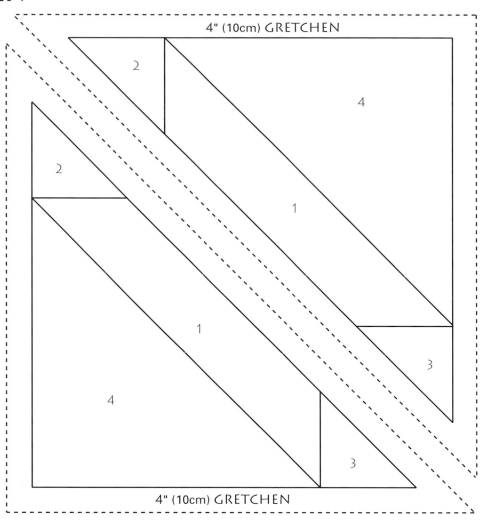

4" (10cm) GRETCHEN

4" (10cm) GRETCHEN

Creative option

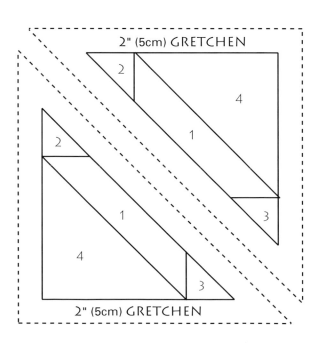

2" (5cm) GRETCHEN

2" (5cm) GRETCHEN

HOURGLASS

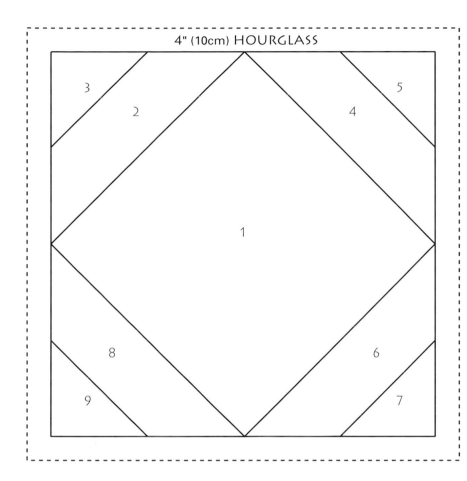

4" (10cm) HOURGLASS

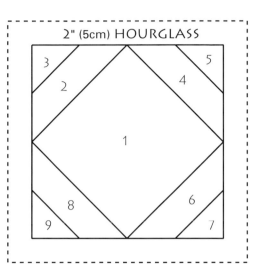

2" (5cm) HOURGLASS

Creative option

DOUBLE PINWHEEL

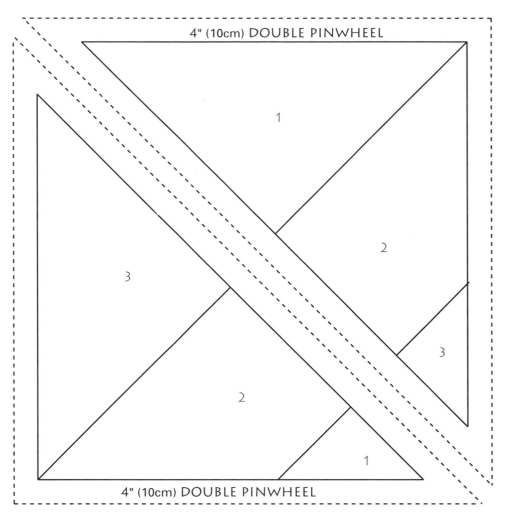

4" (10cm) DOUBLE PINWHEEL

4" (10cm) DOUBLE PINWHEEL

Creative option

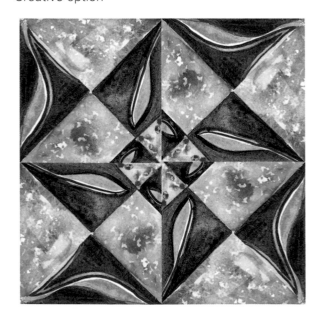

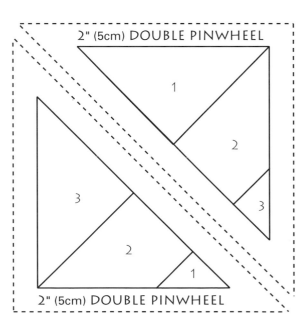

2" (5cm) DOUBLE PINWHEEL

2" (5cm) DOUBLE PINWHEEL

PATRIOTIC FEVER

Red, white, and blue has always been a favorite color scheme in American history. Quilters today, as in the past centuries, can express their political and patriotic sentiments in fabric with these designs.

BALLOT BOX ◆

When American women stitched this block, they had patriotic fever, but not the vote. Make this block and celebrate the triumphs of our suffragette foremothers.

KING'S CROSS ◆◆

Choose striking fabrics for this favorite traditional block to bring out the overall design. Experiment with block layouts—there are some interesting variations.

ROMAN CANDLE ◆◆

This is an easy pattern for making at least two types of stars. What patriotic celebration would be complete without fireworks to brighten the sky?

VICTORY ◆◆

A more complicated version of Roman Candle, this pattern has an exciting sense of movement. Experiment with layouts, as you can make many different stars.

MARINER'S STAR ◆ TO ◆◆◆

Made singly, this pattern yields a crisp, graphic sailboat. Joined together into a star as shown, it can yield exciting dimensional results.

OLD GLORY ◆

No patriotic quilt would be complete without the flag. Traditional color choices will yield the beloved favorite; more contemporary fabrics can infuse sharp "arty" flavor to your quilt.

FLYING PINWHEEL ◆◆

Use bright colors to make this pinwheel star spin inside its framing border triangles. This makes an excellent scrap quilt.

BALLOT BOX

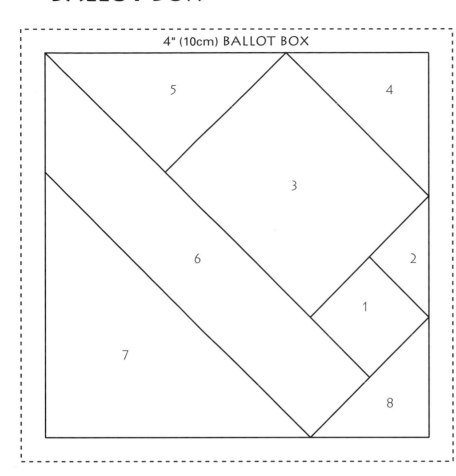

4" (10cm) BALLOT BOX

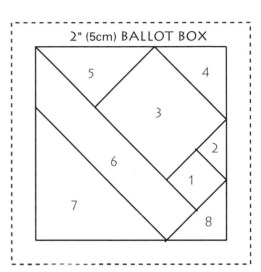

2" (5cm) BALLOT BOX

Creative option

KING'S X

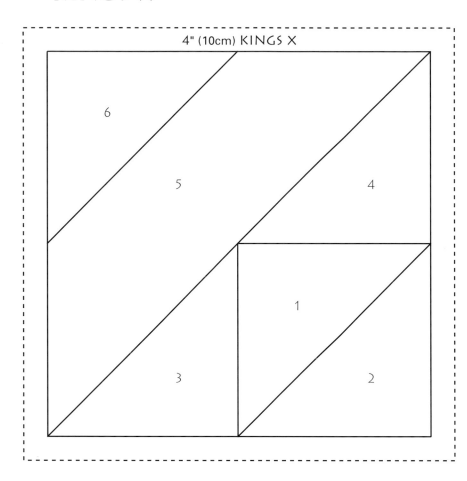

4" (10cm) KINGS X

6

5

4

1

3

2

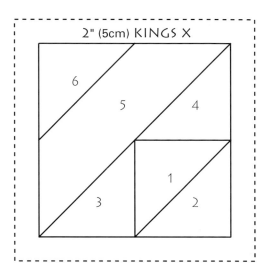

2" (5cm) KINGS X

6

5

4

3

1

2

Creative option

ROMAN CANDLE

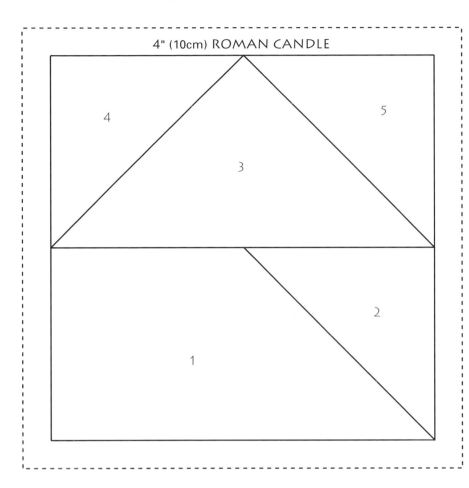

4" (10cm) ROMAN CANDLE

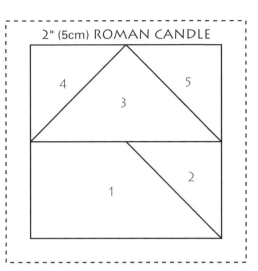

2" (5cm) ROMAN CANDLE

Creative options

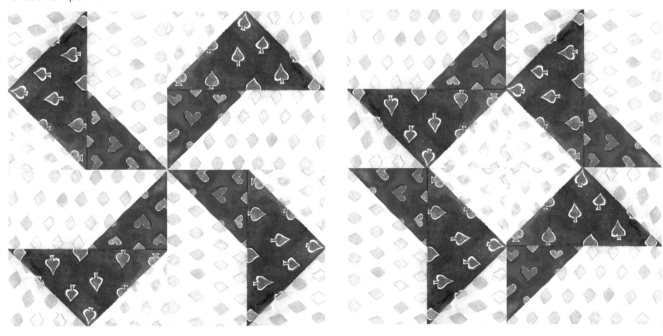

VICTORY

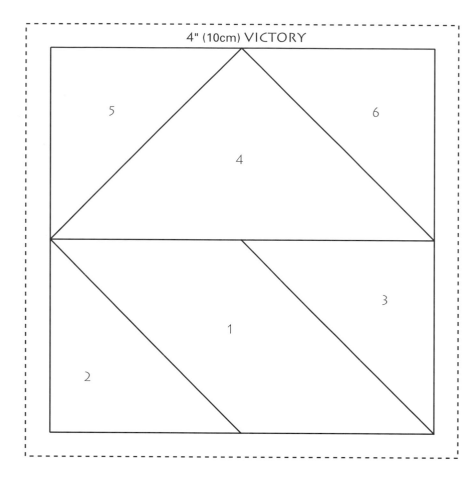

4" (10cm) VICTORY

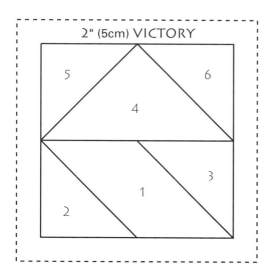

2" (5cm) VICTORY

Creative option

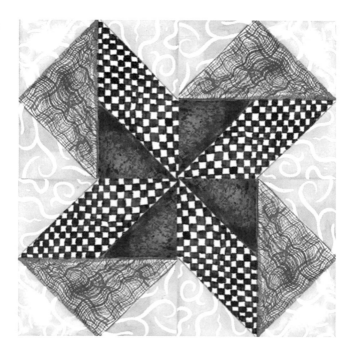

FLYING PINWHEEL

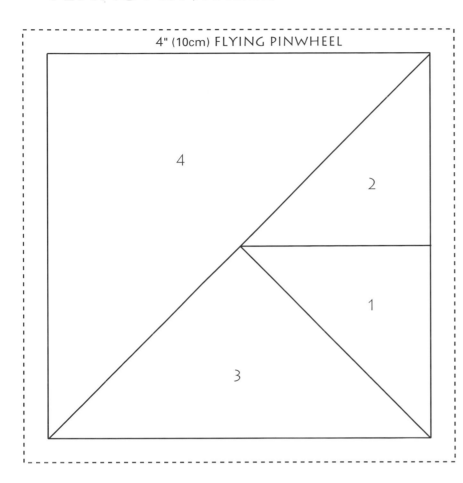

4" (10cm) FLYING PINWHEEL

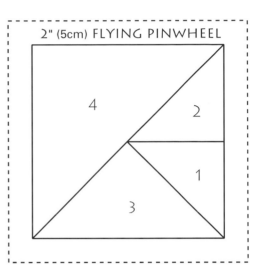

2" (5cm) FLYING PINWHEEL

Creative option

MARINER'S STAR

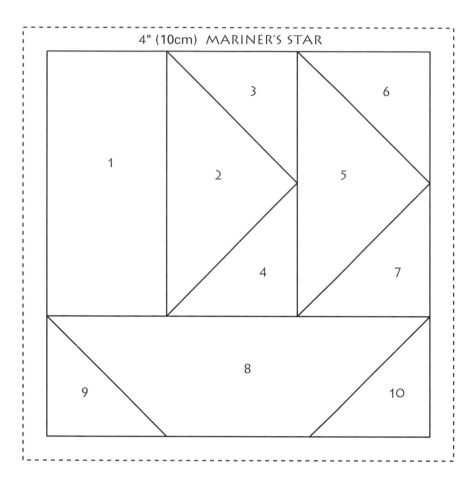

4" (10cm) MARINER'S STAR

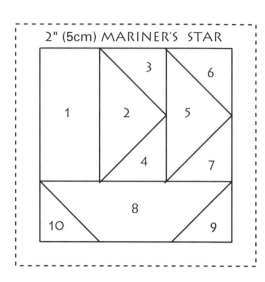

2" (5cm) MARINER'S STAR

Creative option

OLD GLORY

4" (10cm) OLD GLORY

1 RED	
2 WHITE	
3 RED	5 BLUE STARS
4 WHITE	
6 RED	
7 WHITE	
8 RED	

2" (5cm) OLD GLORY

1 RED	
2 WHITE	5 BLUE
3 RED	STARS
4 WHITE	
6 RED	
7 WHITE	
8 RED	

Creative option

WESTWARD HO!

The Victorian era continued the great westward expansion in America and the settlement of Australia, Canada, and New Zealand in the Crown Colonies. Many were the partings of loved ones and the hardships of the pioneer life; it is fitting that needleworkers chose patchwork blocks that commemorated their journey. Select one of these patterns to recapture that pioneer vigor in your quilts.

WHICH WAY SOUTH ◆◆

This block is a variant of the popular Flying Geese motif. Consider it to make a pretty scrap quilt.

OH SUSANNAH ◆

This simple block was first published by the Ladies Art Circle around 1900. It makes a wonderful variety of different patterns, depending on the block orientation in the assembly layout. The traditional name recalls the song of that era, still popular today.

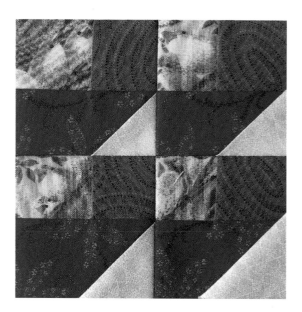

THUNDERBIRD ◆

This block pays homage to the various Native American peoples who were displaced by the westward pioneer movements. Use the layouts shown, or play with the blocks to create your own design.

INDIAN TRAIL ◆◆

This easy traditional block with its strong geometrics can result in very graphic art quilts. It can be an effective scrap quilt as well.

TALL PINE TREE ◆

Was the designer of this pattern thinking longingly of the woods back home as she sewed in her new prairie surroundings, or celebrating the stupendous firs of the Pacific Northwest? This pattern offers the modern quilter ample opportunity for scrap play and graphic results.

TURKEY TRACKS ◆

A prickly variation of the original block, this pattern gives plenty of opportunity for color and layout play.

ROCKY ROAD TO KANSAS ◆◆

This pattern is as old as wagon trains and pioneer brides. Enjoy the string piecing and use up your tiny, much-loved and hoarded scraps.

WHICH WAY SOUTH

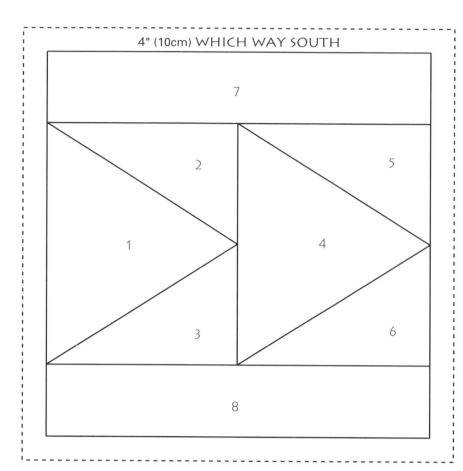

4" (10cm) WHICH WAY SOUTH

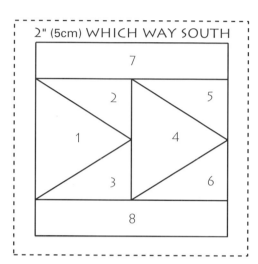

2" (5cm) WHICH WAY SOUTH

Creative option

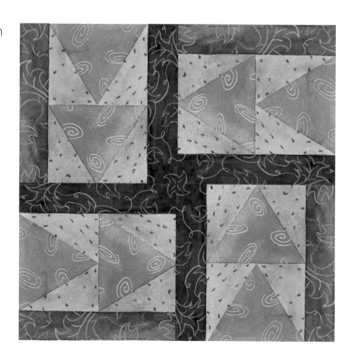

OH SUSANNAH

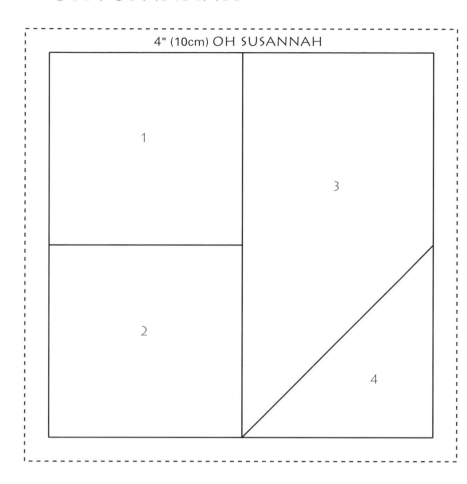

4" (10cm) OH SUSANNAH

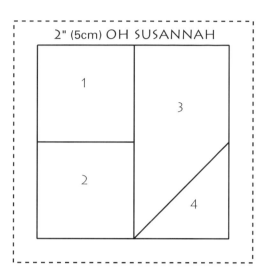

2" (5cm) OH SUSANNAH

Creative options

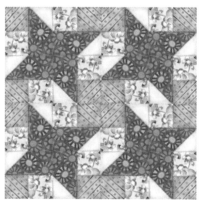

THUNDERBIRD

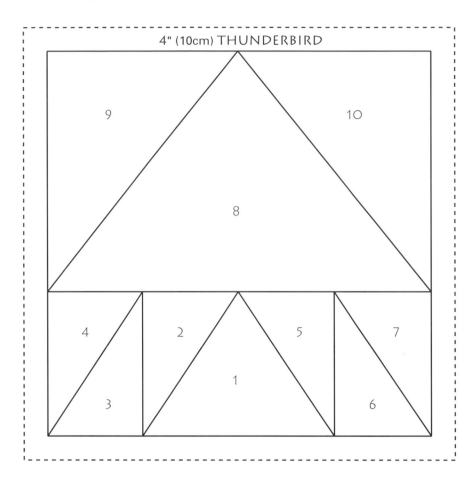

4" (10cm) THUNDERBIRD

9   10

8

4   2   5   7

1

3   6

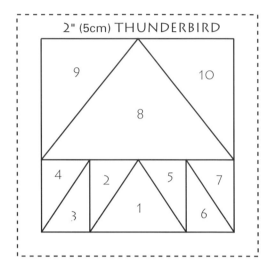

2" (5cm) THUNDERBIRD

9   10

8

4   2   5   7

3   1   6

Creative options

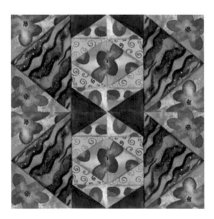

INDIAN TRAIL

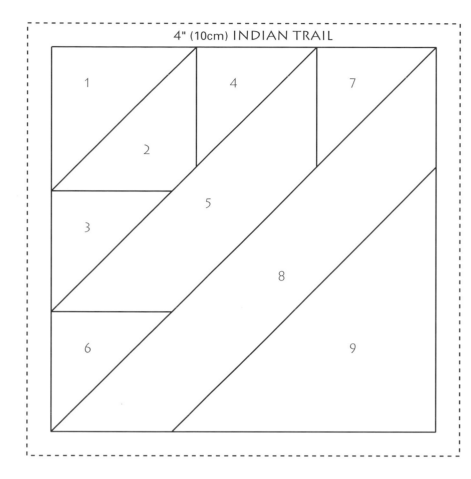

4" (10cm) INDIAN TRAIL

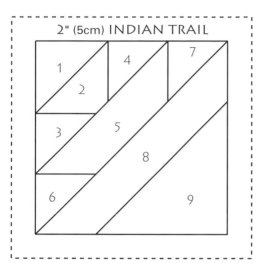

2" (5cm) INDIAN TRAIL

Creative options

TURKEY TRACKS

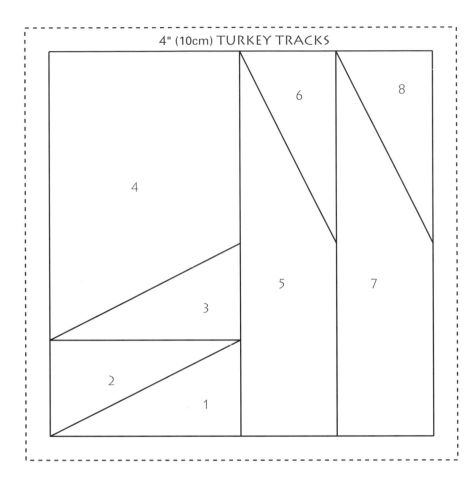

4" (10cm) TURKEY TRACKS

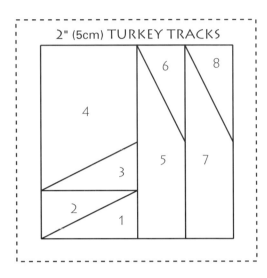

2" (5cm) TURKEY TRACKS

Creative options

TALL PINE TREE

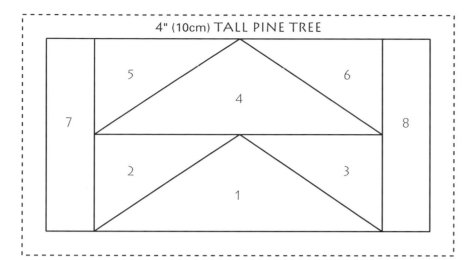

4" (10cm) TALL PINE TREE

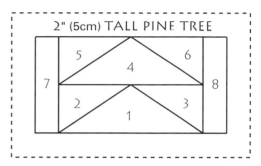

2" (5cm) TALL PINE TREE

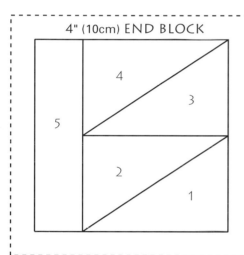

4" (10cm) END BLOCK

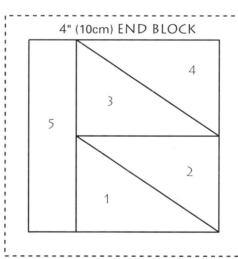

4" (10cm) END BLOCK

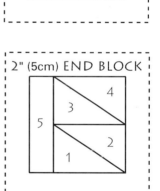

2" (5cm) END BLOCK

2" (5cm) END BLOCK

Creative option

ROCKY ROAD TO KANSAS

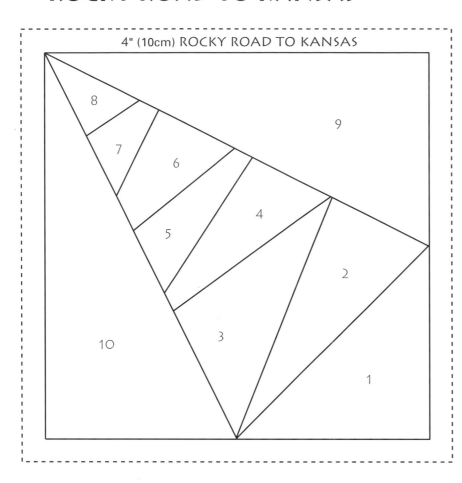

4" (10cm) ROCKY ROAD TO KANSAS

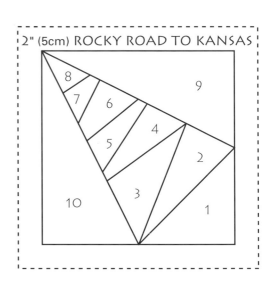

2" (5cm) ROCKY ROAD TO KANSAS

Creative option

FOND MEMORIES

With people moving more frequently due to westward expansion and the Industrial Revolution, separations and partings became more common to Americans. Friendship blocks and quilt exchanges were ways to cling to loved ones far away. Today's quilters may also wish to create personalized commemorative gifts. Signatures should be in permanent ink, or heat-set for permanence. Use the paper foundation to trace a centered name, sentiment, or drawn motif.

FOND MEMORY ◆ TO ◆◆◆

This block is based on a modified sailboat motif and yields a nice framing square for signatures or a rotating star for sets of names. Choose background colors carefully for signature clarity.

FRIENDSHIP CHARM ◆

Based on a very simple traditional pattern, this makes an excellent friendship exchange block. Get together with a group of your quilting friends and exchange either fabric scraps or signed blocks.

PICTURE FRAME ◆

Refer to Jean Ray Laury's book, *Imagery on Fabric*, for a variety of methods available for color or "antique" style photo prints on fabric. Alternatively, you can frame a favorite fabric motif or rubber-stamp image.

DIAMOND MEMORIES ◆◆

A more complex framing pattern, this block in a
4" (10cm) version (or larger) still gives ample space
for featuring favorite photos or images on your quilt.

FRIENDSHIP AUTOGRAPH ◆

This is a very simple but popular traditional autograph
pattern. Make several to exchange with your quilting
friends or make blanks to be signed by family mem-
bers at the next reunion or celebration.

ALBUM ◆

A beloved Victorian era pattern, this block design
offers room for autographs or photo memories. An
excellent scrap quilt opportunity as well.

REMEMBRANCE ◆

A beautiful scrap friendship pattern, this block was
taken from a quilt made for Betsy Wright Lee in the late
1800s. (You can read about Betsy's life and see her quilt
in Linda Otto Lipsett's book, *Remember Me.*) This, too,
makes an excellent block to exchange.

FOND MEMORY

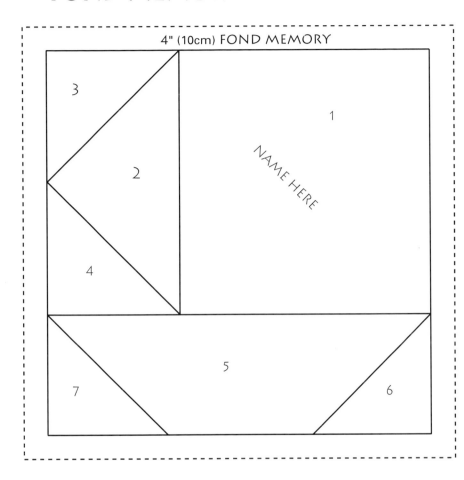

4" (10cm) FOND MEMORY

3

1

2

NAME HERE

4

5

7

6

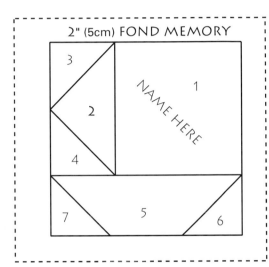

2" (5cm) FOND MEMORY

3

1

2

NAME HERE

4

7

5

6

Creative options

FRIENDSHIP CHARM

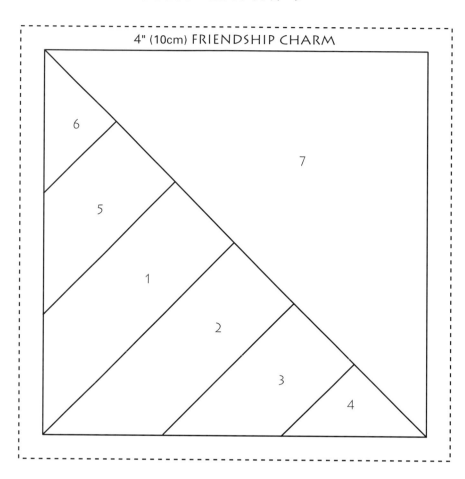

4" (10cm) FRIENDSHIP CHARM

6
5
1
2
3
4
7

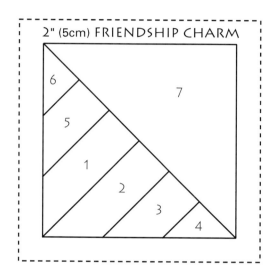

2" (5cm) FRIENDSHIP CHARM

6
5
1
2
3
4
7

Creative options

PICTURE FRAME

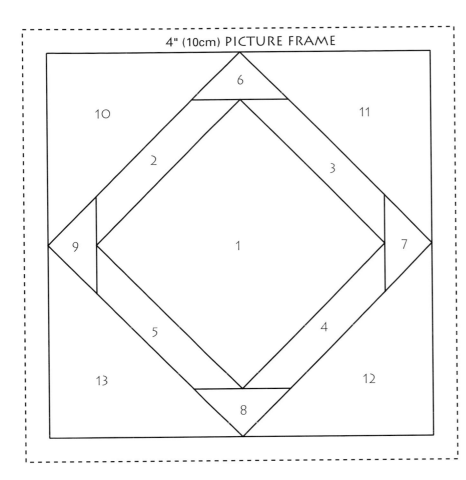

4" (10cm) PICTURE FRAME

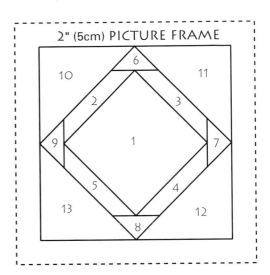

2" (5cm) PICTURE FRAME

Creative option

DIAMOND MEMORIES

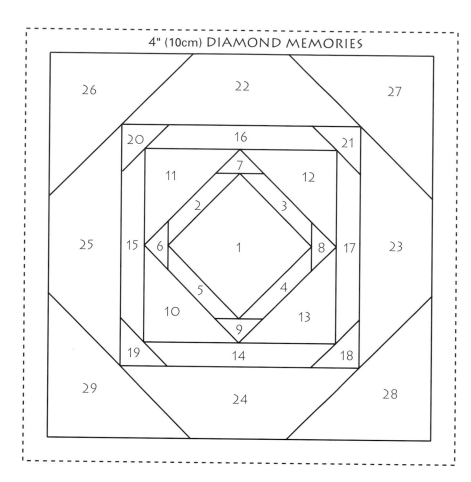

4" (10cm) DIAMOND MEMORIES

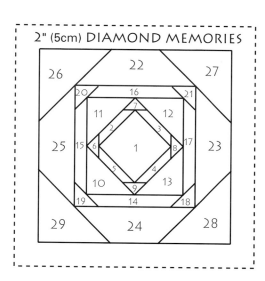

2" (5cm) DIAMOND MEMORIES

Creative option

FRIENDSHIP AUTOGRAPH

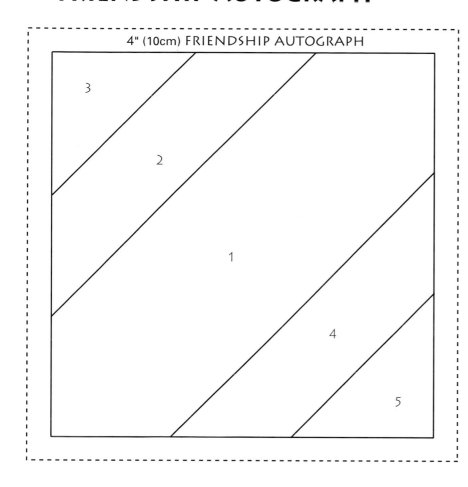

4" (10cm) FRIENDSHIP AUTOGRAPH

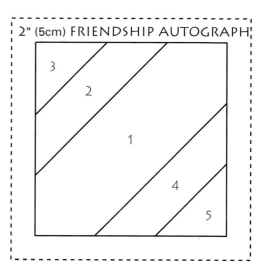

2" (5cm) FRIENDSHIP AUTOGRAPH

Creative options

ALBUM

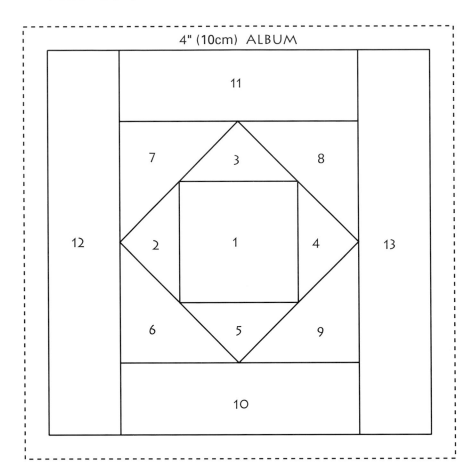

4" (10cm) ALBUM

	11	
7	3	8
12	2 1 4	13
6	5	9
	10	

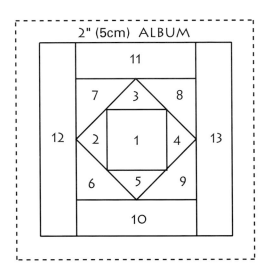

2" (5cm) ALBUM

	11	
7	3	8
12	2 1 4	13
6	5	9
	10	

Creative option

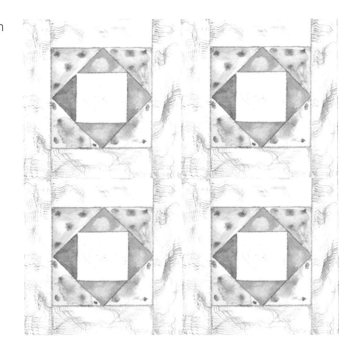

REMEMBRANCE

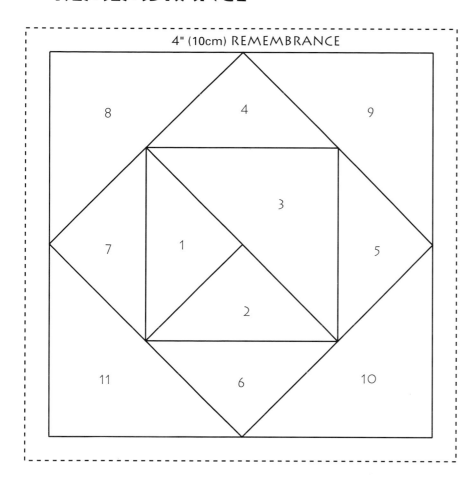

4" (10cm) REMEMBRANCE

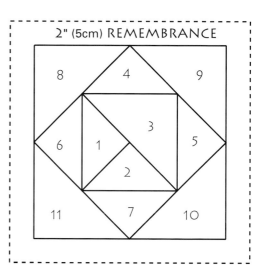

2" (5cm) REMEMBRANCE

Creative option

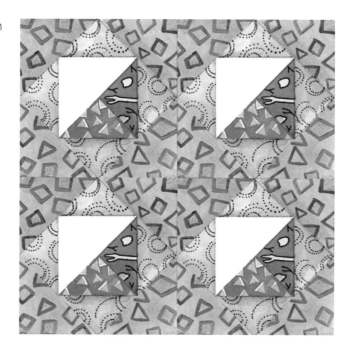

CABINS AND SILKS

The log cabin pattern has been a traditional favorite for more than a hundred years. Victorian women made many variations of this pattern, some in beautifully colored silks and satins using the new bright (almost garish to modern tastes) aniline dyed fabrics. Here are several versions of that theme.

TUMBLING SQUARES ◆

This slightly asymmetrical pattern could be used just as well for another photo-framing design. It is effective in either scrap or coordinated color layouts.

VANISHING WELL ◆

This is a rather straightforward block, though asymmetrical. It combines the classic log cabin and pineapple techniques. Careful color choice will yield a tunnel effect. Experiment with quilt layout designs: there are many exciting possibilities for an overall pattern.

CABIN GEESE ◆

This variant of pineapple log cabin was taken from an antique quilt made in 1890, shown in Kiracofe's

The American Quilt. Choose a striking color for the corner triangles—the geese—to enhance diagonal movement in your quilt.

PATIENCE ◆

This is a simplified version of the log cabin design. You can use striped fabrics for the "logs" so it seems like there are more of them.

SHOWOFF PINEAPPLE ◆◆◆

Adding diagonal rows of ever-increasing triangles brings a sense of movement to this log cabin. Careful color placement will yield some exciting circular shapes. There are numerous pieces to this block, but the construction is straightforward.

SHOWOFF LOG CABIN ◆◆◆

Log cabin quilts have been popular for more than a hundred years. Traditionally, the center square (#1) is red or yellow, and logs are alternately light and dark. Many beautiful arrangements or variations arise due to the placement of light versus dark. This particular block will display your careful construction, which is made much easier by foundation piecing.

TUMBLING SQUARES

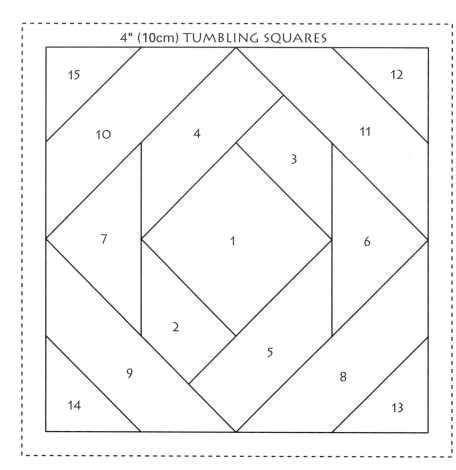

4" (10cm) TUMBLING SQUARES

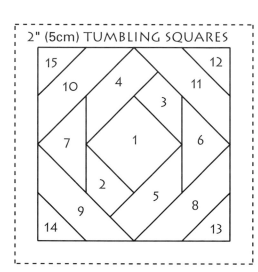

2" (5cm) TUMBLING SQUARES

Creative options

VANISHING WELL

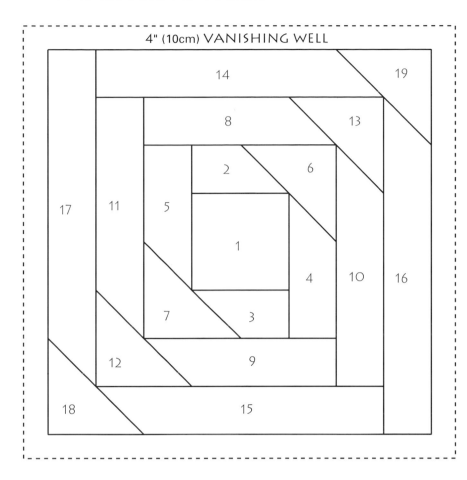

4" (10cm) VANISHING WELL

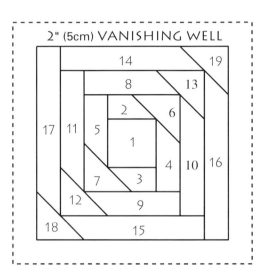

2" (5cm) VANISHING WELL

Creative options

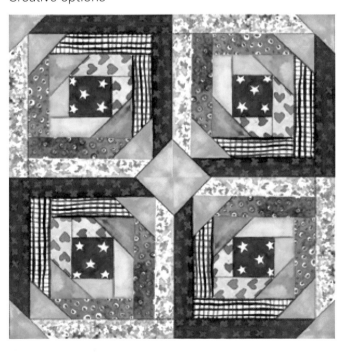

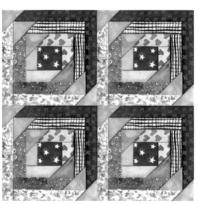

CABIN GEESE

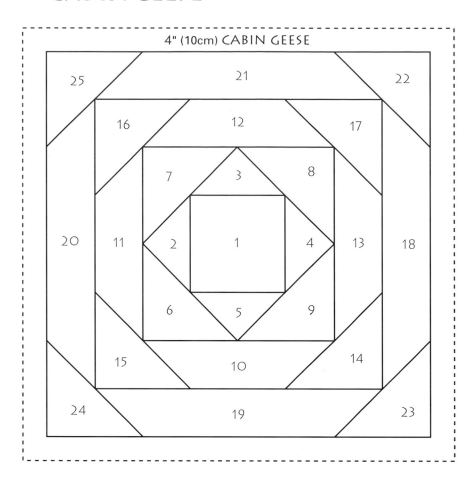

4" (10cm) CABIN GEESE

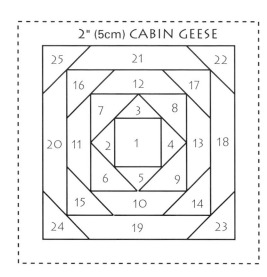

2" (5cm) CABIN GEESE

Creative option

PATIENCE

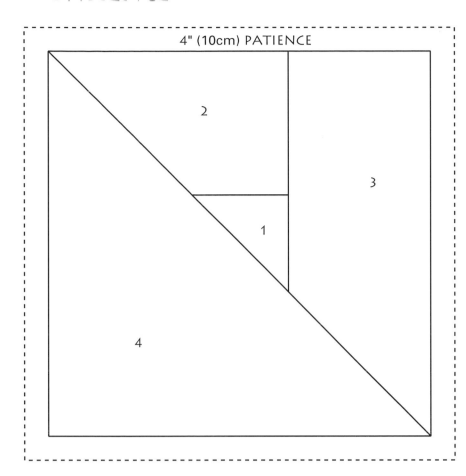

4" (10cm) PATIENCE

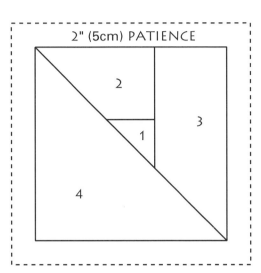

2" (5cm) PATIENCE

Creative option

SHOWOFF LOG CABIN

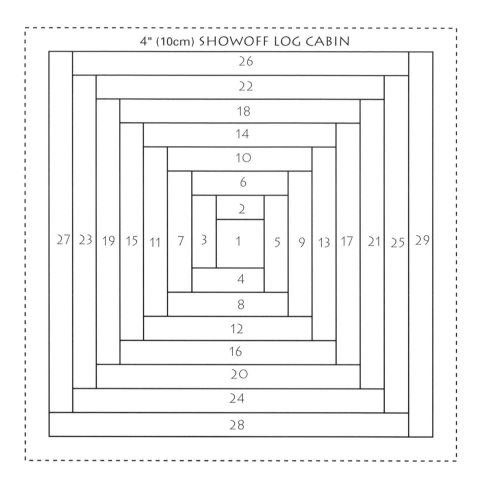

4" (10cm) SHOWOFF LOG CABIN

Creative option

SHOWOFF PINEAPPLE

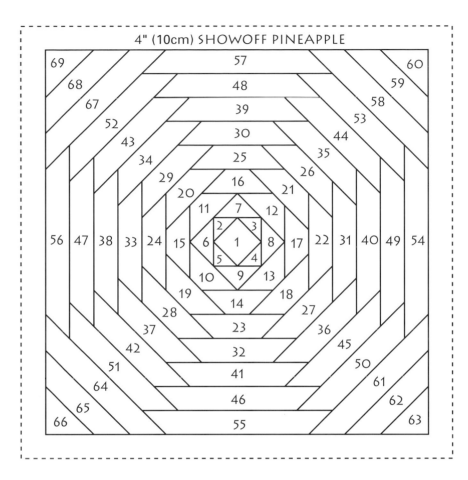

4" (10cm) SHOWOFF PINEAPPLE

Creative option

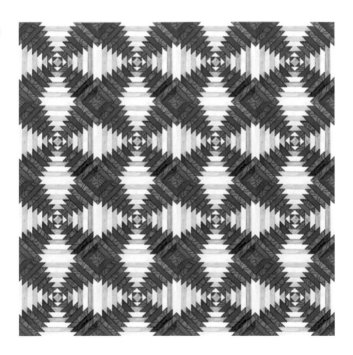

EQUILATERAL TRIANGULAR BORDER

HALF SQUARE
TRIANGULAR BORDER

FRAME BORDERS

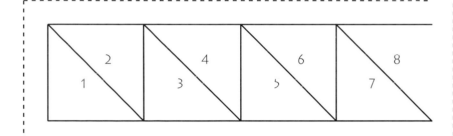

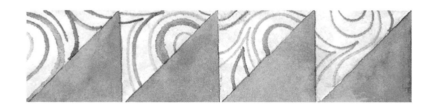

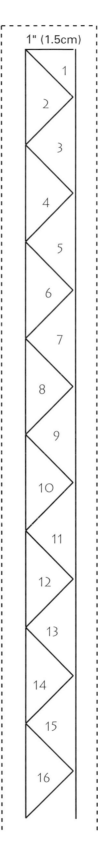

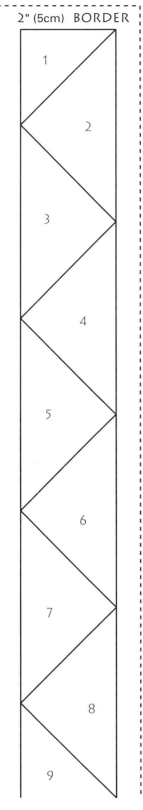

2" (5cm) BORDER

1" (1.5cm)

♦ CHAPTER THREE ♦

QUILT DESIGNS

THE QUILTS

Here are twelve miniature quilt designs, each using one or more of the designs from the block library. Use these quilts as a starting point for your journey into foundation piecing. An easy way to begin is to choose nine blocks, make them up in coordinating fabrics, then stitch them together to make a sampler quilt. This is a great way to try several block designs and gain proficiency at foundation piecing at the same time.

Foundation piecing needn't be limited to miniature quilts. You can enlarge the blocks to make a full-size quilt of 8" (20cm) blocks; for an even larger quilt, add more blocks to the design.

Besides its simplicity, one of the beauties of foundation piecing is the opportunity it presents to use small amounts of leftover fabrics—a scrap saver's dream come true! The quilts shown here generally require less than ¼ yard (22.5cm) of any one fabric, most much less.

Linda's quilts show just a few of the many ways each of the quilt designs can be used. From scrap quilts comprised of dozens of fabrics to two-color quilts of beautiful simplicity, the options are endless.

Many make wonderful two-color quilts, which are especially striking. Pairings of red and white or navy and white, which are traditional choices, are always winning combinations. For a sharp-looking quilt, choose black fabrics teamed with whites. Or, for an unusual quilt, team black with tans or with light grays. For a charming scrap quilt, use this two-color theme by choosing scraps from the two chosen colors. Don't be too worried about having all the colors perfectly matched; if your navy blues vary in intensity, the finished quilt will have that much more character.

Yet another option is to use two prints in two shades of one color. Pair a red with a pink or a forest green with a lighter green. To add a twist, find a green print with a little pink flower in it for your quilt and bring the pink to life by adding a pink binding.

For more of a challenge, try a three-color quilt. The green and red coupled with white makes Spring Song sparkle. A bit of gold in the brown fabric together with the vibrant red and sobering off-white present a striking setting for the sepia fabric photo transfer blocks of Memory Album. Here a taste of a fourth color is added in one of the three major prints, adding that perfect touch. In Independence Day, Linda followed the three-color theme, but this time she added a second shade of blue and stenciled the inner square.

Several of these quilts are true scrap quilts. Crazy patch is a prime example. Notice that Linda used many different fabrics in her crazy quilt, but the quilt maintains its integrity. Each block contains certain colors that unify the quilt: a red, a dark green and a secondary green, a purple, a pink, and a brown. The remaining patches repeat the colors, but not the fabrics. Though these aren't always the same (for example, red fabrics block to block) the colors and feel of the fabric are very much the same, and therefore are connected. The pink and purple in each block marry the blocks to the pink and purple border and the brown quilt binding. The patches of teacup fabric in most (not all—don't want to be too predictable!) of the blocks appear random, but further unify the quilt and add just the right bit of whimsy.

Another traditional scrap quilt, Geese by the Cabin, is a variation on the popular Log Cabin design. This time Linda chose specific fabrics for her quilt rather than the scrap effect. Though her fabric selections make the design appear tricky, a quick study will show otherwise. Make a copy of the pattern and assign a number to each of the fabrics. You'll find the design is actually quite simple.

Fabric requirements are specified for all the quilts. These represent the amounts Linda used. Fabric usage can vary depending upon cutting efficiency, so be sure to purchase a little extra fabric. Remaining yardage can be used as binding or pieced together for interesting quilt backings.

JODIE DAVIS

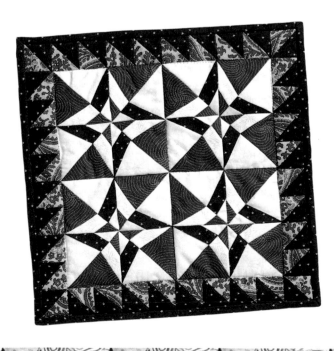

COUNTRY COUSINS QUILT

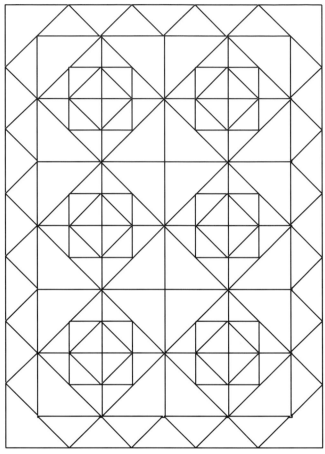

FINISHED SIZE: 10" × 14" (25.5 × 35.5cm)

FABRIC REQUIREMENTS: 1¼ yard (114.5cm) each
of two fabrics

BLOCKS: Two 3" (7.5cm) wide and four 2" (5cm)
wide strips 40" (101.5cm) long for each of
two colors

BORDER: Two 3" (7.5cm) wide strips of each for
two colors

BACKING: 12" × 16" (30.5 × 40.5cm)

BATTING: 12" × 16" (30.5 × 40.5cm)

◆ **COUNTRY COUSINS (page 51)**

2" (5cm) block size

Make 24

◆ **FRAME BORDER (page 97)**

1" (2.5cm) wide

Make 2 to finish 8" (20.5cm) for top and
bottom borders

Make 2 to finish 14" (35.5cm) for side borders
(includes corner pieces)

This design is most effective when it is done
in two colors, such as blue and white, and makes
a wonderful scrap quilt: choose scraps within
two color choices. Fabric requirements are for a
two-color (two-fabric) quilt.

CRAZY QUILT

FINISHED SIZE: 14" × 18" (35.5 × 45.5cm)

FABRIC REQUIREMENTS:

BLOCKS: Scraps of many fabrics

BORDER: Scraps at least 1½" (4cm) wide

BACKING: 16" × 20" (40.5 × 51cm)

BATTING: 16" × 20" (40.5 × 51cm)

♦ **CRAZY PATCH I (page 28)**

    4" (10cm) block size

    Make 3

♦ **CRAZY PATCH II (page 28)**

    4" (10cm) block size

    Make 3

♦ **CRAZY PATCH III (page 29)**

    4" (10cm) block size

    Make 3

♦ **CRAZY PATCH IV (page 29)**

    4" (10cm) block size

    Make 3

♦ **EQUILATERAL TRIANGLE BORDER (page 96)**

    1" (2.5cm) wide

Make 2 to finish 12" (30cm) on the short side and 13" (33cm) on the long (out) side for the top and bottom borders

Make 2 to finish 16" (40.5cm) on the short side and 18" (45.5cm) on the long side (includes corner triangles) for side borders

Crazy Quilt offers an opportunity to use scraps of velveteen, lamé, and other noncotton fabrics. Use a permanent foundation to give the fabrics stability.

DELECTABLE MOUNTAINS QUILT

FINISHED SIZE: 20" × 20" (51 × 51cm)

FABRIC REQUIREMENTS: 1¼ yard (114.5cm) each
of two fabrics

DELECTABLE MOUNTAINS BLOCKS: Three 4"
(10cm) wide strips 40" (101.5cm) long and
seven 1½" (4cm) wide strips 40" (101.5cm)
long for each of two colors (mountains and
background)

BORDER: Five 3" (7.5cm) wide strips 40" (101.5cm)
long for each of two colors

BACKING: 22" × 22" (56 × 56cm)

BATTING: 22" × 22" (56 × 56cm)

♦ **DELECTABLE MOUNTAINS (page 44)**

4" (10cm) block size

Make 16

♦ **HALF SQUARE TRIANGULAR BORDER (page 96)**

2" (5cm) wide

Make 2 strips for top and bottom borders with 4 triangles in one orientation and 4 in the other for
a finished total length of 16" (40.5cm) each

Make 2 strips for the side borders with 5 triangles in
one orientation and 5 in the other for a total finished length of 20" (51cm) each (includes corner blocks)

This pattern works best when done in two colors, or as a scrap quilt within these color choices.

GEESE BY THE CABIN QUILT

FINISHED SIZE: 14" × 14" (35.5 × 35.5cm)

FABRIC REQUIREMENTS:

BLOCKS: Scraps 1½" (4cm), 3" (7.5cm), and 5"
(13cm) wide in dark- and light-colored "logs"

One 1½" (4cm) wide strip for the center blocks,
traditionally red or yellow

BORDER: Four strips 3" (7.5cm) wide and
40" (101.5cm) long each of dark colors
and of background

BACKING: 16" × 16" (40.5 × 40.5cm)

BATTING: 16" × 16" (40.5 × 40.5cm)

◆ **CABIN GEESE (page 92)**

4" (10cm) block size

Make 9

◆ **FRAME BORDER (page 97)**

1" (2.5cm) wide

Make 2 to finish 12" (30cm) long for top and
bottom borders

Make 2 to finish 14" (35.5cm) for sides (includes
corner block)

This pattern looks best if the corner "geese"
triangles are all the same color. It makes a wonderful scrap quilt in light and dark fabrics.

INDEPENDENCE DAY QUILT

FINISHED SIZE: 11⅝" × 11⅝" (29.5 × 29.5cm)

FABRIC REQUIREMENTS:

CENTER: 3" × 3" (7.5 × 7.5cm) square of fabric

OLD GLORY BLOCKS: One 2" × 8" (5 × 20.5cm) scrap of blue

One 5" × 12" (13 × 30cm) scrap of red

One 5" × 10" (13 × 25.5cm) scrap of white

ROMAN CANDLE BLOCKS: Two 3" (7.5cm) wide strips 40" (101.5cm) long of blue

Two 5" (13cm) wide strips 40" (101.5cm) long of red

One 5" (7.5cm) wide strip 40" (101.5cm) long of white

Three 3" (7.5cm) wide strips 40" (101.5cm) long of white

OUTER BORDER: Two strips 1" × 12½" (2.5 × 31.5cm) and two strips 1" × 14½" (2.5 × 37cm) of blue

BACKING: 14" × 14" (35.5 × 35.5cm)

BATTING: 14" × 14" (35.5 × 35.5cm)

♦ **ROMAN CANDLE (page 65)**

4" (10cm) block size

Make 4 (sixteen 2" [5cm] subunit block foundations)

♦ **OLD GLORY (page 69)**

4" (10cm) block size

Make 4

Add a personal touch to the center block with a rubber-stamped or stenciled patriotic image or ink signature, or use a figured fabric.

INDIAN TRAILS QUILT

FINISHED SIZE: 18" × 18" (45.5 × 45.5cm)

FABRIC REQUIREMENTS:

BLOCKS: For longest strip: One piece 6" (15cm) wide and 25" (63.5cm) long

For medium strip: One piece 4" (10cm) wide and 25" (63.5cm) long

For short strip: One piece 2½" (6.5cm) wide and 25" (63.5) long

For background: Two strips 3½" (9cm) wide and 40" (101.5cm) long

Four strips 2" (5cm) wide and 40" (101.5cm) long

BORDER: Four strips 3" (7.5cm) wide and 40" (101.5cm) long of each of two colors

BACKING: 20" × 20" (51 × 51cm)

BATTING: 20" × 20" (51 × 51cm)

♦ **INDIAN TRAIL (page 75)**

4" (10cm) block size

Make 16

♦ **FRAME BORDER (page 97)**

1" (2.5cm) wide

Make 2 to finish 16" (40.5cm) long

Make 2 to finish 18" (45.5cm) long with corner pattern

MEMORY ALBUM QUILT

FINISHED SIZE: 13" × 13" (33 × 33cm)

FABRIC REQUIREMENTS:

Fond Memory blocks: Scraps 1½" (4cm) wide for
small triangles (brown in photograph)

One 2½" (6.5cm) wide strip 40" (101.5cm) long for
large triangle

One 3" (7.5cm) wide strip 40" (101.5cm) long for
pinwheels (red in photograph)

One 2" (5cm) strip 40" (101.5cm) long for background

Picture Frame blocks: Scraps 1½" (4cm) wide for
small triangles

One strip 2½" (6.5cm) wide for frame

Two 3" (7.5cm) wide strips 40" (101.5cm) long for
corner triangles

Five 2½" × 2½" (6.5 × 6.5cm) squares for picture
frame center

BORDER: Four 1" × 13½" (2.5 × 34.5cm) strips

Scraps for corners

BACKING: 15" × 15" (38 × 38cm)

BATTING: 15" × 15" (38 × 38cm)

◆ **PICTURE FRAME (page 83)**

4" (10cm) block size

Make 5

◆ **FOND MEMORY (page 81)**

4" (10cm) block size

Make 4 (sixteen 2" [5cm] subunit foundations)

Use photo transfer medium to add photographs
to the fabric squares inside the picture frame blocks.

NIGHT AND DAY QUILT

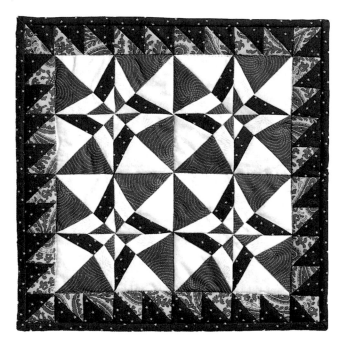

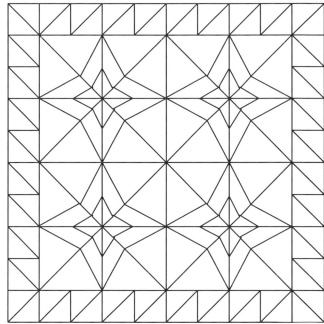

FINISHED SIZE: 10" × 10" (25.5 × 25.5cm)

FABRIC REQUIREMENTS:

BLOCKS: Strips 1½" (4cm) wide and 1½" (4cm),

2½" (6.5cm), and 3½" (9cm) long of dark and

light fabrics

BORDER: Two strips 1½" (4cm) wide and 40"

(101.5cm) long of dark and light fabrics

BACKING: 12" × 12" (30 × 30cm)

BATTING: 12" × 12"(30 × 30cm)

♦ **NIGHT AND DAY (page 57)**

4" (10cm) block size

Make 4

♦ **HALF SQUARE TRIANGULAR BORDER (page 96)**

1" (2.5cm) wide

Make 2 to finish 12" (30cm) long

Make 2 to finish 14" (35.5cm) long (to include corners)

This is another striking two-color quilt. For a
more subtle effect, use a monochromatic theme:
choose two shades of a color, such as a dark and
light blue.

ORIENTAL WONDER QUILT

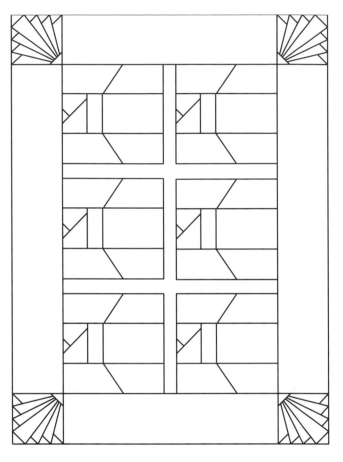

FINISHED SIZE: 12½" × 17" (31.5 × 43cm)

FABRIC REQUIREMENTS:

Kimono blocks: Strips 1½" (4cm) and 2½" (6.5cm) wide and 1½" (4cm) wide for kimono

Samurai Fan blocks: Scraps of six fabrics

SASHING: Three rectangles 1" × 4" (2.5 × 10cm) to join block horizontally and two rectangles 1" × 9" (2.5 × 23cm) to join vertically

BORDER: Two rectangles 2½" × 9" (6.5 × 23cm) for top and bottom borders and two rectangles 2½" × 13½" (6.5 × 34.5cm) for side borders

BACKING: 15" × 19" (38 × 48cm)

BATTING: 15" × 19" (38 × 48cm)

♦ **KIMONO (page 32)**

4" (10cm) block size

Make 6

♦ **SAMURAI FAN (page 35)**

2" (5cm) block size

Make 4

PINEBURR BEAUTY QUILT

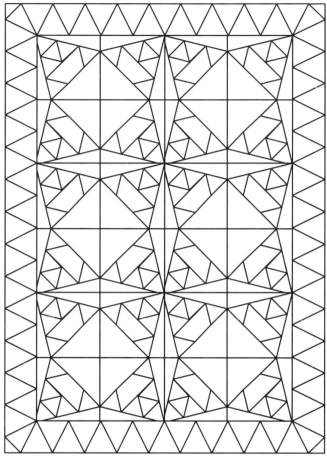

FINISHED SIZE: 10" × 14" (25.5 × 35.5cm)

FABRIC REQUIREMENTS:

BLOCKS (in colors as shown in photograph):

One 2" (5cm) wide strip 40" (101.5cm) long

in dark green

Two 1½" (4cm) wide strips 40" (101.5cm) long in

light green

Two 2" (5cm) wide strips 40" (101.5cm) long in

purple

Two 2½" (6.5cm) wide strips 40" (101.5cm) long in

off-white (background)

BORDER: Two 2" (5cm) wide strips 40" (101.5cm)

long of two colors

BACKING: 12" × 16" (30 × 40.5cm)

BATTING: 12" × 16" (30 × 40.5cm)

♦ **PINEBURR BEAUTY (page 42)**

4" (10cm) block size

Make 6 (24 2" [5cm] subunit foundations)

♦ **EQUILATERAL TRIANGULAR BORDER (page 96)**

1" (2.5cm) wide

Make 2 to finish 8" (20.5cm) long

Make 2 to finish 8" (20.5cm) long (plus corner blocks)

SPRING SONG QUILT

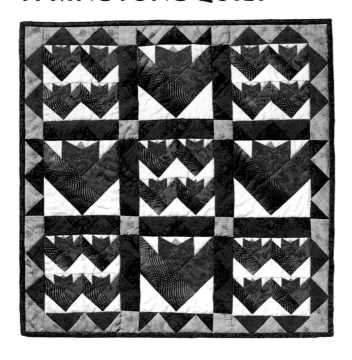

FINISHED SIZE: 16" × 16" (40.5 × 40.5cm)

FABRIC REQUIREMENTS:

4" (10cm) BLOCKS: One strip 3" (7.5cm) wide and 40" (101.5cm) long in red

One strip 2" (5cm) wide and 40" (101.5cm) long in green

One strip 3" (7.5cm) wide and 40" (101.5cm) long in white

2" (5cm) BLOCKS: Two strips 2" (5cm) wide and 40" (101.5cm) long in red

Two strips 2½" (6.5cm) wide and 40" (101.5cm) long in green

Two strips 2" (5cm) wide and 40" (101.5cm) long in green

BORDER AND SASHING: Three strips 3" (7.5cm) wide and 40" (101.5cm) long in red

Two strips 3" (7.5cm) wide and 40" (101.5cm) long in dark green

Three strips 3" (7.5cm) wide and 40" (101.5cm) long in light green

BACKING: 18" × 18" (45.5 × 45.5cm)

BATTING: 18" × 18" (45.5 × 45.5cm)

♦ **CROCUS (page 43)**

2" (5cm) block size

Make 20

♦ **CROCUS (page 43)**

4" (10cm) block size

Make 4

♦ **FRAME BORDER (page 97)**

2" (5cm) wide

Make 12 sashing strips in dark green and red with light green corner blocks

Make 2 borders to finish 14" (35.5cm) long and 2 to finish 16" (40.5cm) long, the latter to include the corners, following the photograph for color placement

TALL PINE TREES QUILT

FINISHED SIZE: 11" × 14" (28 × 35.5cm)

FABRIC REQUIREMENTS:

BLOCKS: 2½" (6.5cm) wide strips in green for tree greenery

One 3" (7.5cm) wide strip 40" (101.5cm) long in brown for tree trunks

Two 2½" (6.5cm) wide strips 40" (101.5cm) long in blue for background

One 2½" (6.5cm) wide strip 40" (101.5cm) long in green for outside left and right blocks

BORDER: Two strips 1¾" × 11½" (4.5 × 29cm) each for top and bottom borders

BACKING: 13" × 16" (33 × 40.5cm)

BATTING: 13" × 16" (33 × 40.5cm)

♦ **TALL PINE TREE (page 77)**

4" (10cm) block size

Make 9

♦ **TALL PINE TREE (page 77)**

End block 4" (10cm) wide

Make 3 half-blocks

♦ **TALL PINE TREE (page 77)**

End block 4" (10cm) wide

Make 3 half-blocks (mirror image)

Block D is a 1" × ½" (2.5cm × 12mm) strip.

Block E is the end block without piece 5. Make 6.

Make 3 mirror pieces as well.

◆ CHAPTER FOUR ◆

FINISHING

This chapter contains instructions for completing your quilt top, making the quilt "sandwich," binding your quilt, and adding a sleeve for hanging. Refer to the general quilting titles listed in the bibliography for thorough discussions of these topics as well as excellent books on machine quilting.

JOINING THE BLOCKS

Lay out the blocks according to the layout diagram for the quilt you are making. Beginning at the top left corner, match the adjoining sides of the first two blocks, right sides together. Place a pin through seams that need matching. Baste ¼" (6mm) from the raw edge, as marked on the foundation. Check to be sure seams match and points meet, where necessary. Stitch.

Keep adding blocks until you have completed the top horizontal row. Do the same for each remaining row. Press seam allowances open. Stitch the rows together, carefully matching seams. Press seam allowances open.

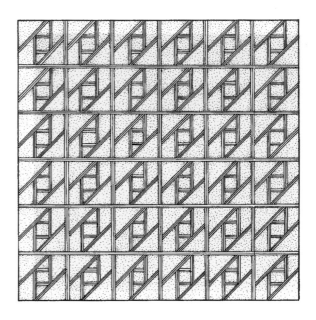

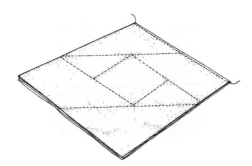

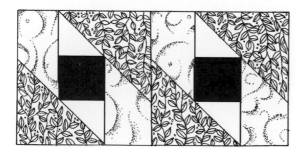

If you've removed the paper foundation before quilt assembly, use spray sizing on your completed blocks before assembling them. This makes them easier to handle and produces smoother looking seams.

ELLEN ROBINSON
GERMANTOWN, MD

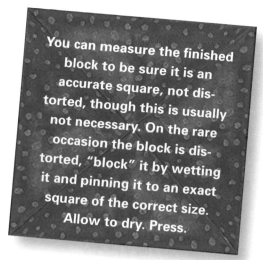

You can measure the finished block to be sure it is an accurate square, not distorted, though this is usually not necessary. On the rare occasion the block is distorted, "block" it by wetting it and pinning it to an exact square of the correct size. Allow to dry. Press.

NOTE: Some block patterns include strategic points that must match when the rows are stitched. In this case I baste the blocks together, check the alignment, and then stitch when I'm satisfied that they match up properly.

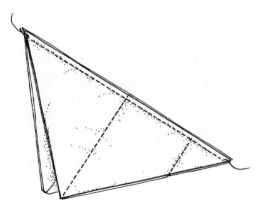

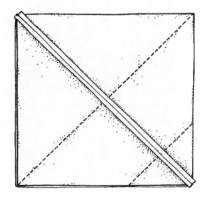

REMOVING THE PAPER

If you used paper as the foundation for your quilt, gently tear the paper from the backs of the blocks now, as if you were tearing stamps. Press the blocks gently, lifting the iron up and down rather than dragging it, so as not to distort the blocks.

Paper removal can be somewhat tedious when working with a completed top—you may find a good pair of tweezers helpful in the task.

For fabric foundations, you can use cotton yardage you no longer want for piecing. Be sure there is no show-through from the print.

For paper foundations: after sewing two blocks together, pull the paper from the seam allowance. This will enable you to press the seam allowances flat and makes for easier paper removal when the quilt top is complete.

BASTING AND QUILTING

Now your quilt top is ready to be made into a quilt.

1. Cut the batting and backing about 1" (2.5cm) larger all around than the quilt top.

2. Lay the backing wrong side up on a large, flat surface.

3. Lay the batting on top.

4. Lay the quilt top, right side up, centered on top of the backing and batting.

5. Working from the center out, thread or safety-pin baste the three layers of the quilt "sandwich" together.

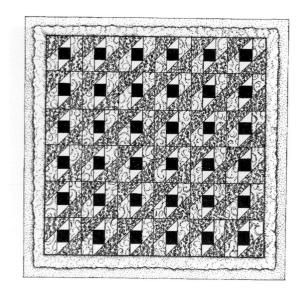

6. Quilt as desired.

7. Remove all basting stitches or remaining safety pins.

> Use masking tape for a precise, easy-to-follow straight-line quilting pattern. Be sure to remove the tape immediately after quilting so it won't leave a sticky residue.

BINDING

You may bind your quilt—finish the outer edges with fabric—by either folding the backing to the front and stitching in place, or adding a separate strip of fabric.

NOTE: While they make a perfectly acceptable finish for a wall quilt, self-bindings may not be the best choice for a bed quilt. For these, use an attached binding strip. The double thickness of fabric in this type of binding will better withstand the wear and tear of everyday use.

SELF-BINDING

1. Trim the batting even with the quilt top. Trim the backing to ¾" (2cm) larger than the outer edge of the quilt all around.

2. Along one edge, fold the backing ¼" (6mm) to the front. Fold the backing to the front, over the edges of the batting and quilt top. Fold the sides in first, and slip-stitch by hand or topstitch by machine. Repeat at top and bottom.

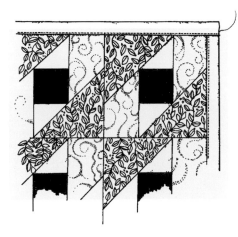

ATTACHED BINDING

1. Trim the batting and backing so that they are even with the quilt top.

2. To determine how long a binding to make, add the measurements of the four sides of your quilt top and an extra 8" (20cm).

3. Cut strips of binding along the straight, crosswise grain (there is some give to the crosswise grain) of your fabric. Use a diagonal seam to piece the strips together if necessary.

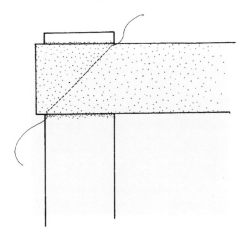

NOTE: The width of your binding strips is determined by the size of your quilt. For a wall hanging–size quilt, the finished binding that shows on the front surface should be about ¼" (6mm). The larger size of a bed quilt requires a binding ½" (12mm) or wider for proper proportion. As an easy rule of thumb, cut your binding strips 1¾" (4.5cm) wide for wall hangings and 3¼" (8cm) wide for bed quilts.

4. Wrong sides together, fold the seamed strips lengthwise in half. Press.

5. From right side and matching raw edges, place the binding strip along one edge of the quilt top. Machine-stitch the binding to the quilt "sandwich," using a ¼" (6mm) or ½" (12mm) seam allowance, depending on the desired finished binding width. Leave the first 3" (7.5cm) or so of the binding unstitched so you can join the two ends of the binding later.

For a quilt-show quality finish, join the ends of the binding one-third away from the lower right-hand edge of the quilt. This is the least noticeable join location and is the choice of award-winning quilters.

6. At the first corner, stop stitching ¼" (6mm) or ½" (12mm), according to your seam allowance, from the edge of the quilt top. Raise the presser foot, but leave the needle down, in the fabric.

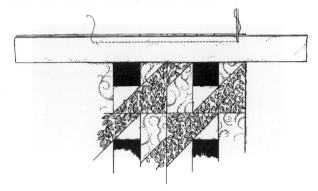

Pivot, and stitch diagonally to the corner of the quilt and off.

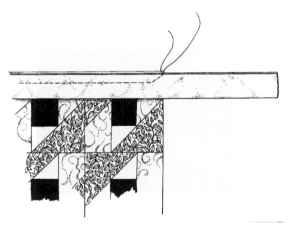

Hold the binding so the loose end is straight up from the next side.

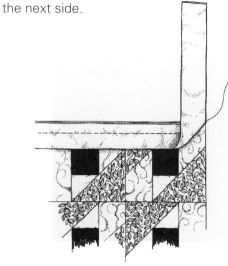

Fold the loose binding down, matching the raw edge to that of the next side of the quilt, and sew to the next corner.

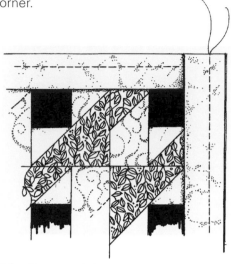

Repeat for the remaining corners.

7. When you approach about 4" (10cm) of the beginning of the binding, stop stitching. Match the ends of the binding as shown, opening them up to stitch them together along the diagonal. Refold and finish sewing the seam.

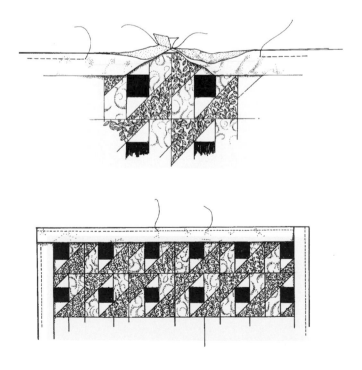

8. Fold the binding to the back of the quilt over the raw edges of the quilt "sandwich," covering the machine stitching at the back of the quilt. Slip-stitch the binding in place.

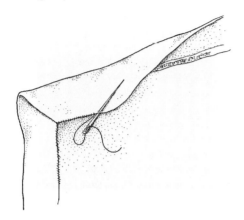

> To build a fabric collection quickly, look for fat quarters at your local quilt store. Fat quarters are one-half of ½ yard (45.5cm) of fabric and measure 18" × 22" (45.5 × 5cm). Fat eighths are also often available. Also, mail-order suppliers (see Sources) carry scrap bags of remnants and precut square assortments.

ADDING A HANGING SLEEVE

To hang a quilt on a wall, sew a simple sleeve to the back. A rod or ⅜" (9mm) to ¾" (2cm) dowel slipped into the sleeve provides the support to hang your quilt nicely. Cut the dowel 1" longer than the sleeve.

1. Cut a strip of fabric 3½" wide and as long as the width of your quilt less 1" (2.5cm) to 2" (5cm). Press

each short end ¼" (6mm) to the wrong side twice. Topstitch.

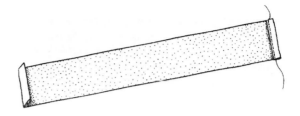

2. Wrong sides together, fold the sleeve strip lengthwise in half. Center the raw edge of the strip along the top edge of the back of the quilt before attaching the binding. Baste.

3. Stitch the binding to the quilt as instructed above, securing the sleeve in the seam.

4. Slip-stitch the bottom, folded edge of the sleeve to the back of the quilt.

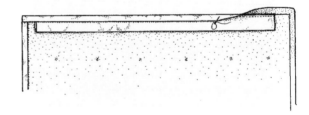

> Identify your quilt with a label. Include your name, the name of the design, date completed, and any other pertinent information.

YOU ARE INVITED...

One of the greatest pleasures in what I do is meeting people who share the quilting passion. Seeing the incredible quilts these talented souls create and sharing the joy of quilting is inspiring and invigorating.

In this spirit, please share your creations with me through the mail or via one of the online services. Whether you use the designs in this book or any other, use these ideas as a springboard for your creativity, or embark on your own creative endeavors. I'd love to see what you're making. I look forward to meeting you.

JODIE DAVIS

Jodie Davis Publishing, Inc.
15 West 26th Street
New York, NY 10010

or via email: CompuServe: 73522,2430
GEnie: J.DAVIS60

SOURCES

CLOTILDE

2 Sew Smart Way

Stevens Point, WI 54481

(800) 772-2891

Catalog: Free

Sewing and quilting supplies.

KEEPSAKE QUILTING

Route 25B

P.O. Box 1618

Centre Harbor, NH 03226-1618

(603) 253-8731

Catalog: Free, or $1.00 for first-class mail

Pigma pens, books, fabric, huge selection of quilting supplies.

PURCHASE FOR LESS

231 Floresta

Portola Valley, CA 94028

Catalog: $2.00

Quilt books at discounted prices.

QUILTS & OTHER COMFORTS

1 Quilters Lane

P.O. Box 4100

Golden, CO 80401-0100

(800) 881-6624

Catalog: Free

Books, large selection of quilting supplies.

THE QUILTER'S BOOKSHELF

3244 N. Hackett Avenue

Milwaukee, WI 53211

Catalog: $2.00 (refundable)

Exhaustive forty-eight-page catalog of more than four hundred quilt books.

BIBLIOGRAPHY

The following books are all excellent quilting references and welcome additions to the quilter's bookshelf.

Fanning, Robbie, and Tony Fanning. *The Complete Book of Machine Quilting*. 2nd ed. Radnor, Pa.: Chilton Book Company, 1994.

Fones, Marianne, and Liz Porter. *Quilter's Complete Guide*. Birmingham, Ala.: Oxmoor House, 1993.

Hargrave, Harriet. *Heirloom Machine Quilting*. Lafayette, Calif.: C&T Publishing, 1990.

Singer Sewing Reference Library. *Quilting by Machine*. Minnetonka, Minn.: Cy DeCosse Inc., 1990.

Thomas, Donna Lynn. *A Perfect Match: A Guide to Precise Machine Piecing*. Bothell, Wash.: That Patchwork Place, 1993.

REFERENCE

For more information about American quiltmaking history, refer to the following books.

Brackman, Barbara. *Clues in the Calico.*

Kiracofe. *The American Quilt.*

Laury, Jean Ray. *Imagery on Fabric.*

Lipsett, Linda Otto. *Remember Me.*

INDEX